MW01258664

DAYTON
BEER

DAYTON BEER

A HISTORY OF BREWING
IN THE MIAMI VALLEY

 TIMOTHY R. GAFFNEY

AMERICAN PALATE

Published by American Palate
A Division of The History Press
Charleston, SC
www.historypress.com

Copyright © 2019 by Timothy R. Gaffney
All rights reserved

First published 2019

Manufactured in the United States

ISBN 9781467138925

Library of Congress Control Number: 2019937036

Notice: The information in this book is true and complete to the best of our knowledge. It is offered without guarantee on the part of the author or The History Press. The author and The History Press disclaim all liability in connection with the use of this book.

All rights reserved. No part of this book may be reproduced or transmitted in any form whatsoever without prior written permission from the publisher except in the case of brief quotations embodied in critical articles and reviews.

CONTENTS

PREFACE

Every book is a journey of discovery for its author, and so this one was for me. I learned the beer of our forefathers, like local craft beer now, reflected the life experiences of its brewers and the history of the region where it was made—not only human history but also the natural history that shaped the land and the local climate. I learned the story of beer in the Miami Valley is entwined with stories about the birth of America, the displacement of native people, the struggles of immigrants, the building of canals and railroads and even the terraforming work of glaciers. I learned much of the history of our early brewers and their breweries is all but lost, scattered among thousands of records and a few precious collections preserved by archivists, librarians and historical society volunteers—bless them all. As I pored over census sheets, land records, birth, marriage and death certificates, passport applications, Civil War registries and obituaries, some brewers seemed to come to life, transfiguring familiar streets with their breweries and homes, while others remained elusive spirits. Still, I learned how some of them lived and, in a few cases, how they died.

Citations are important, but it would have been impractical to cite every record I consulted. Besides the usual history books, newspaper microfilms and city directories, I tapped ancestry databases to review thousands of census, marriage, birth, death, cemetery and land records.

Misspellings of immigrants' names are common in historical records, and sometimes they changed their names over time. Records of their places of origin were often vague, conflicting or illegible. Also, digitized indexes of genealogical databases sometimes misinterpreted spellings in the original, handwritten records. I used the names and spellings the individuals themselves or their descendants seemed to prefer, but I noted alternate spellings in cases where it wasn't conclusive.

ACKNOWLEDGEMENTS

I thought writing a book about the history of beer brewing in the Miami Valley would be as easy, and almost as quick, as homebrewing a batch of ale. I was wrong. I owe a huge debt of gratitude to my wife, Jean, for carrying on without complaint while I spent endless hours at my computer, in archives and, of course, in brewpubs. I thank my acquisitions editor, John Rodrigue, and Senior Editor Ryan Finn. Many others provided information and pictures or helped me dig up records. Thanks to Jann Kuehn Adams, Jamie Arthur, Steve Barnhart, Adam Becker, Tanya Brock, Brad Bergefurd, Nate Cornett and Lisa Wolters, Mark Fisher, Natalie Fritz (and Clark County Historical Society), Brenda Gibson (and Miami Conservancy District), Janine Kohlhorst Gulich, Karla Hollencamp, Nancy Horlacher (and Dayton Metro Library), Angie Hoschouer (and Historic Woodland Cemetery and Arboretum), Mindy Kannianen, Justin Kohnen, Vickie Lockwood, Kevin Loftis, the volunteers of Minster Historical Society, Nick Moeller, Rick Ordeman (and Miami Valley chapter, Brewery Collectibles Club of America), Jeff Puterbaugh, Jim Sachs, Dr. David Schmidt, Shelby County Historical Society, Kyle Spears (and Dayton History), Linda Trent (and Troy Historical Society), Jack Waite, Sharon Watson (and Piqua Public Library) and Mackensie Wittmer (and Oakwood Historical Society).

INTRODUCTION

A visitor to the Miami Valley in the 1850s would have found a variety of breweries, some of wood and some of brick, their rooms filled with oak barrels and plank tables. On a cold day, hearths with blazing logs would have banished the chill.

A typical brewing works would have been a gravity-fed system mounted on its own brick superstructure along one wall. A flight of rough steps would have led up to a large kettle over a wood fire—a course the brewer's apprentices would have known all too well from hauling up countless armloads of firewood and buckets of water. The brewing process would have gone like this: From the kettle, heated water drained into a lower kettle, called a mash tun, to soak floor-malted grains the brewer had roasted in an open hearth and stone ground in a hand-cranked grinder. From the mash tun, the resulting wort drained into another open kettle, to be boiled and flavored with hops and spices, and then circulated through a coiled pipe in a barrel filled with ice-cold water before finally arriving, unfiltered, in a fermenting barrel. After a week, the young beer would be drained into another barrel to rest for two weeks, aging and clarifying.

In Dayton, such a brewery stands today. Dayton History, a nonprofit historical society, joined the craft beer movement in 2014 in its own unique way: by building an authentic, 1850s-style brewery based on local research and using traditional materials and methods. The brick-and-timber building is set in Carillon Historical Park, a sixty-five-acre, open-air museum of restored and replica buildings where authentically costumed

Carillon Brewing Company at Carillon Historical Park. *Author's collection.*

staff and volunteers bring the region's history to life through interpretation and programs. At Carillon Brewing, visitors can watch brewers in period costume make beer while they dine on German-themed food. For a fee, one can be "brewer for a day," suiting up in period clothes and working with the head brewer to learn the historical process of beer making. Carillon Brewing calls it "History by the Pint."

As of this writing, the head brewer is Kyle Spears, a historian who dabbled in homebrewing during his college years. In 2018, four years after joining Dayton History, Spears said he enjoyed telling visitors about Dayton's brewing heritage as much as practicing the craft.

This melding of craft beer with local history is a distinctive feature of the craft beer movement sweeping the Miami Valley as of this writing. In numerous interviews and conversations for this book, craft brewers in the Dayton region described their businesses as part of the larger movement toward locally grown and manufactured goods. They tap history to accentuate

Kyle Spears, head brewer at Carillon Brewing. *Dayton History.*

the local nature of their goods in a variety of ways, from repurposing old buildings to branding their products with names from Dayton's past. Beer lovers can down a pint named for Xenia's Hollencamp family of brewers or Dayton's once popular Superba brand or drink any number of beers named for famous Dayton inventors and inventions. "I think people want to be connected to their community," Spears said.

As the following pages show, the history of brewing in Dayton is bound up in the larger history of the region, going back to its earliest people and even the earth under our feet.[1]

CHAPTER 1

GEORGE NEWCOM'S DAYTON BREWERY

No matter how it's brewed, every beer made in the Miami Valley shares these ingredients: more than 2 million years of glaciers and 12,000 years of human history.

Before the first brewers arrived, glaciers up to a mile thick bulldozed much of Ohio, grinding up rock and filling ancient river valleys with layers of sand and gravel, which then filled with water to become aquifers. Ample rainfall made clean water an abundant, easily accessible resource—witness towns named for water, such as Springboro, Springfield and Yellow Springs. The Great Miami and Little Miami Rivers formed paths that became primary transportation arteries, eventually augmented by canals, railroads and highways.

People started moving into the region as the most recent glacier retreated, about twelve thousand years ago. The first settlers left stone spear points and, later, complex ceremonial earthworks and burial mounds. In the seventeenth century, French explorers found a land rich with timber, game and water, as well as villages whose people had called the land home for centuries. England and France fought for control of the rich Ohio country. England prevailed, but then rebellious colonists claimed the territory for their new country, America.

The young federal government defined a vast area of wilderness north and west of the Ohio River as the Northwest Territory, and it set rules for settlement—never mind those already living there. In the late 1700s, the once quiet forests of the Ohio country rang with gunfire as the resident people battled encroaching foreigners. In 1793, General Anthony Wayne (known as "Mad Anthony" for his daring Revolutionary War tactics) built a series of forts in western Ohio. In August the following year, his army defeated a force of Native Americans in the Battle of Fallen Timbers, near where Toledo would rise. The defeat compelled them to sign the 1795 Treaty of Greenville, which opened the door to settlers who took the land for themselves.

The treaty's ink was barely dry when Israel Ludlow laid out the site for Dayton in November 1795, according to Robert W. and Mary Davies Steele's *Early Dayton*. Ludlow named the town for Jonathan Dayton, a Revolutionary War general and one of the original purchasers of the townsite. The first settlers came by way of Cincinnati in March 1796. One of their leaders was Colonel George Newcom (1771–1853), an Irish immigrant who had served in Wayne's army. Newcom and his family quickly built a rough, one-room cabin at the southwest corner of Main and Monument Streets and then hired a millwright to build a proper, two-story house. In the winter of 1798–99, he made the house into a tavern by doubling its size, according to A.W. Drury's *History of the City of Dayton*.

Newcom's Tavern was a hewn-log structure made with windows, chinked with lime mortar, equipped with a large stone fireplace and topped off with

Newcom's Tavern in Carillon Historical Park. *Author's collection.*

a small belfry. It was downright palatial compared to the humble cabins around it. The Steeles described it as "the pride of all this region on account of its superiority to any other house north of Hamilton." It served as store, church, courthouse and hotel.

In 1809 or 1810, Newcom built Montgomery County's first brewery of record next to the tavern. He operated it until about 1811 or 1816—accounts differ—when a Robert Graham took over the tavern for several years.

The brewery is long gone, but Newcom's Tavern survived to become a cherished local landmark. Moved and restored twice, after 1964 it stood in Dayton History's Carillon Historical Park, about two miles from its original site and a short walk from Carillon Brewing.

The Dayton Brewery and John W. Harries

Montgomery County's first brick brewery went up in about 1820, Drury wrote. It was the work of Henry Brown (circa 1770–1825), a Virginia native who was in the business of trading with Native Americans. He built Dayton's first store on Main Street in 1804. In 1808, he built Dayton's first brick house, a two-story dwelling on the west side of Main Street between Second and Third. Brown's brewery stood on the south side of Second Street west of Jefferson. He owned the brewery only a short time, and he's better known for other things, including an old cannon he dubbed "Mad Anthony." Being Dayton's only cannon at the time, it was the ceremonial artillery piece for every occasion deserving of a thunderous salute. Townsfolk hauled it out of Brown's barn and fired it for years until one day the barrel burst, killing the gunner, according to the Steeles.

Brown's establishment became known as the Dayton Brewery under the next two owners, James L. Morris and Michael Ott. In 1828, Drury wrote, George C. Davis moved it to a new building on the west side of Jefferson Street, midway between First and Monument. It continued to produce beer, porter and ale for nearly half a century as Dayton evolved from a pioneer settlement into a mature city. Parking lots bracketing an alley occupy the site as of this writing.[2]

The man most responsible for the Dayton Brewery's long-running success was John W. Harries (1783–1873), an immigrant farmer from the Welsh county of Carmarthenshire. Harries came to New York with his family in 1823. He worked there as a grocer until 1829, when he brought his family to

Lock 27, a restored lock of the Miami and Erie Canal below Miamisburg. *Author's collection.*

Dayton. They came by way of Cincinnati aboard the canalboat *Experiment*. They were among the first travelers on the new Miami and Erie Canal, which had just opened to Dayton that year.

Ohio built the canal between Cincinnati and Toledo as a way to connect its settlers with eastern markets. The north end gave access to the East Coast via the Great Lakes and the Erie Canal. Goods traveling south went down the Ohio and Mississippi Rivers to ports in New Orleans.

The canal also became an important conduit for settlers like Harries, who found in Dayton a bustling town that was doubling its population every decade. Nearly three thousand people lived there in 1830, more than double the number from a decade earlier, and growth continued to surge through the end of the century, when Dayton's population reached eighty thousand.

Brewing is an ancient practice in Wales, but it didn't mean Harries had secret Welsh recipes up his sleeve. He was new to the craft. He plunged into it "notwithstanding his means were limited as well as his knowledge of the business," as local historian Frank Conover wrote in *Centennial Portrait and Biographical Record of the City of Dayton and Montgomery County, Ohio*. But what Harries lacked in knowledge and experience, he made up for with "perseverance and considerable native ability," Conover noted. Harries acquired the Dayton Brewery and ran it successfully until his death. He ended life as a wealthy man: his estate records listed houses and properties all over town and in Illinois and Indiana, not to mention cash, stocks and other valuables. He left the brewery and two malting houses, among other things, to his son, Charles.

Location of John W. Harries brewery. *From* Combination Atlas Map of Montgomery County, Ohio *(1875)*.

Charles Harries (1827–1907) had been involved in the brewing business since at least 1850, according to census records. But his father's luck didn't seem to transfer with the brewery: he owned it only four years before it closed in 1877, according to Robert A. Musson's *Brewing Beer in the Gem City*.[3]

RIDDLE, FERNEDING AND THE CITY BREWERY

James Riddle was another pioneer brewer. His record is as murky as the ales he likely brewed. Local history books barely mention him, but he started what would become one of Dayton's longest-lasting breweries. Riddle (circa 1788–1855) hailed from somewhere in Pennsylvania, according to the 1850 census. He was married to Isabella Mead (circa 1793–1875). Her obituary in the *Dayton Journal* revealed James served with the Mounted Rangers in the Indiana wilderness during the War of 1812. After his discharge, Riddle must have decided it was time for a beer—a lot of it. He moved to Dayton and opened a brewery.

It's unclear exactly when Riddle arrived. His obituary put it at 1827, but census records show a James Riddle in town as early as 1820. When and where he started brewing is likewise unknown, but a biographical sketch had him in business by 1840. Historical accounts and land records indicate the brewery stood on St. Clair Street near East Third.

Most references to Riddle's establishment turn up in the context of another brewer, Henry Ferneding. Ferneding (1812–1905) was born in Dinklage, a town in what was then the Grand Duchy of Oldenburg (later a district in Lower Saxony, Germany), according to census records and news reports. He came to America around 1833 and lived in Baltimore before moving to Cincinnati and finally settling in Dayton. His biographical sketch in W.H. Beers's *History of Montgomery County, Ohio* notes Riddle employed him in 1840. What's amazing is that Ferneding survived until then.

According to the sketch, Ferneding began his journey to Dayton by walking roughly two hundred miles from Baltimore to Pittsburgh. It doesn't describe the route, but he likely followed the new National Road for much of his trek. From Pittsburgh, he floated down the Ohio River to Cincinnati. There he found work driving a milk wagon, but "being broken down in health," Ferneding came to Dayton to work on the Miami and Erie Canal. He carried water and handed out jiggers of whiskey to the digging crews—not hard work, from the sound of it—but a severe, persistent bout of chills and fever forced him to quit and kept him bedridden for much of the next six months. Whenever he was well enough to work, he sawed wood to make ends meet.

Once he finally recovered, Ferneding found work in the distillery of the brothers Horace and Perry Pease on Hole's Creek until 1839, when he moved forty miles south to Milford for a job in the John Koogler distillery. But bad luck followed, and he again fell ill for two months. Next he moved to Hamilton, thirty-two miles southwest of Dayton, to work in the Huston and Harper distillery. There a slop pipe burst, spraying him with a scalding-hot slurry of spent mash. It took him three months to recover.

Ferneding returned to the Dayton area. He took a job in the Snyder & Dryden distillery, and in 1840 he married Elizabeth Taphorn, who had come from Oldenburg in 1838. He also went to work for Riddle, switching from distilling to brewing.

Joining Henry was his brother, John Casper Ferneding (circa 1805–1851). John was Henry's elder by seven years, but he left a fainter trail in history. It's uncertain whether he traveled to Dayton with his brother or how close they were. The 1840 census put him in Dayton with five others in his household, but it didn't identify other family members or list occupations. By 1850, though, he was living with his presumed wife, Christina, and six-year-old Henry under his brother's roof, and he was working as a brewer.

Land records for Riddle's brewery are confusing, in part because the Fernedings often went by "Fanning" in the early and middle 1800s. (Henry finally set the record straight in 1900 with an affidavit he filed in the county recorder's office.) But the records show Henry and a partner, Frank J. Otten, bought property between St. Clair and Kenton Streets in 1845 and began manufacturing malt, the process of germinating and then drying grains for brewing. Otten died around 1847, and the next year, Henry and his brother, John, acquired what had been Otten's share of the property. Likewise, it isn't known how long Riddle ran his brewery. The 1850 census has him still working as a brewer in the same neighborhood. Harvey W. Crew, in *History of Dayton, Ohio*, wrote the Fernedings "purchased the old Riddle brewery" in 1850 and tore it down to build a new malt house. But they continued to operate a brewery on the east side of Kenton near Third, across from Cooper Park and the future site of the Dayton Metro Library.

After Otten's death, the Ferneding brothers carried on the business as J.&H. Ferneding, but bad luck returned with a vengeance: John died a year later at about forty-six, and of Henry's nine children, all died in their youth but one, Clement Joseph. Clement (1846–1931) joined his father in the malting business for a while, according to biographical, land and census records, but he studied at St. Mary's Institute (later the University of Dayton) and focused on banking and railroads.

Henry picked up a new partner, Bernard Hollencamp, in 1852. They operated as Fanning and Company, brewers and maltsters, and as the City Brewery. They also bought the Xenia Brewing Company from James Kyle in Xenia. It operated as Hollencamp & Company until 1857, when Hollencamp became sole owner and exited Ferneding's business.

In 1859, Ferneding built a new brewery on the west side of Warren Street, just south of Apple and just under a mile south of his old brewery. (The Miami Valley Hospital parking garage occupies the site as of this writing.) He kept the malting business on Kenton but shuttered the old brewery.

More than a simple relocation, Beers wrote, Ferneding was making a strategic move. Dayton's beer market was changing. German immigrants were a growing part of Dayton's population. They brought with them

Homes of Henry (*left*) and Clement J. Ferneding. *From* Combination Atlas Map of Montgomery County, Ohio (*1875*).

something that was beginning to transform brewing in Dayton and across the country: a taste for lager beer. Brewing lager beer required special facilities, and Ferneding saw he would need a new brewery to keep up with the market.[4]

German Immigration and Lager Beer

Brewing is as old as civilization, but different ingredients and practices have produced a wide variety of beers. Early American brewers mainly made ales and porters, and their open kettles allowed wild yeasts from the air to feast on the wort and colonize the fermenting barrels. The result was often sour beer, something Spears admitted was a challenge at Carillon Brewing. Frederick William Salem, a nineteenth-century brewing industry advocate, put it this way in his 1880 book *Beer, Its History and Its Economic Value as a National Beverage*: "Outside the larger cities, even twenty years ago, ale was almost sure to be dull and muddy and very apt to be sour." He might well have been describing the kind of beers Harries and Ferneding served in the 1850s and before.

But fifteenth-century brewers in the Bavarian Alps discovered a kind of yeast that fermented beer slowly in cool conditions. It made a clearer, crisper, palate-pleasing beer. Brewers called the slow fermentation process lagering, a German word for storing, and they called the beer lager.

The process spread in Europe, and it suited the temperate conditions brewers found in America's northern states. Brewers could harvest ice from frozen ponds in winter and use it to refrigerate lagering cellars in summer. While brewers embraced mechanical refrigeration in the late 1800s, *The Western Brewer*'s 1901 supplement, *One Hundred Years of Brewing*, described numerous U.S. breweries still using natural ice at the turn of the century.

A Bavarian brewmaster named John Wagner is widely credited with bringing the first lager yeast to America in 1840 and setting up a small brewery in Philadelphia. Lager beer spread along the East Coast and made its way inland. Ales were much improved by 1880, Salem wrote, adding, "Now almost anywhere one is certain of a tolerable glass of beer." And he noted the "recent great increase in the use of lager beer."[5]

Given lager beer's rapid growth, it's hardly surprising that it quickly found its way to Dayton. Germans had been coming to the area since the first days of European settlement. German Township was one of Montgomery County's four original townships in 1803, and Germantown was laid out in

1814. By 1850, about one-tenth of all Daytonians were from German states. A U.S. Census survey conducted in 2011 found 16.1 percent of Daytonians identified as being of German descent, and the percentage was even higher in suburban communities—31.3 percent in Kettering and 29.3 percent in Oakwood, for examples.

Like the Pilgrims, many German immigrants came to escape political or religious persecution. Between 1830 and the First World War, nearly 90 percent of all German emigrants chose to settle in the United States, according to a Library of Congress report. A failed revolution in 1848 drove a wave of immigration to the United States. Some of their traditions became widespread, such as the Christmas tree, Santa Claus and Easter eggs.

Cincinnati was a popular destination for German immigrants. Many came overland from eastern ports, such as Philadelphia, to the Ohio River and then down the river to Cincinnati. Others made their way up the Mississippi and Ohio from New Orleans. At Cincinnati, they congregated on the edge of town in an area known as Over-the-Rhine. There, new arrivals found a familiar culture where German language and customs prevailed.

This culture included beer, and German immigrants built Cincinnati into a major brewing center. In 2012, geospatial scientist Samuel A. Batzli at the University of Wisconsin mapped breweries in the United States over the nation's history. From 1640 through 1840, he found Cincinnati placed seventh among U.S. cities in the number of breweries. From 1841 through 1865, the period when German brewers established lager beer in America, Cincinnati rose to fourth. In terms of output, Cincinnati helped make Ohio the nation's third-biggest beer-producing state by the late 1870s. Salem reported Ohio breweries filled more than 968,000 barrels in 1877, following only New York (3,556,678 barrels) and Pennsylvania (1,041,486). Christian Moerlein, an Over-the-Rhine brewer, accounted for nearly 10 percent of Ohio's output with 98,191 barrels—far and away the most by any single Ohio brewer. Many Germans who settled in the Miami Valley above Cincinnati came by way of Over-the-Rhine.

Many in the established population didn't welcome the German newcomers or their lager beer. In *History of the Woman's Temperance Crusade*, Annie Wittenmyer, president of the Woman's Christian Temperance Union, wrote in 1878 that in Dayton, besides "the usual array of saloons, and gambling-dens, and brothels, where liquors were sold and drank," there were "massive breweries, and great wholesale houses, that by their influence and money sustained the traffic; and the business was largely in the hands of a rough class of foreigner, mainly Germans."[6]

THE SCHIMLS

The group Wittenmyer so disdained included the Schimls. Born in Bavaria, John Schiml (circa 1820–1858) came to Dayton in 1845. Whether he was seeking opportunity, escaping oppression or both isn't stated in biographical sketches. His father, Christopher, was "a prominent mill owner, a man of means and commercial standing," according to Beers. But the elder Schiml died in 1842, leaving a widow and eight children. Five of John's siblings also died in the next few years. Whether planned or not, John's immigration made him the vanguard of his family. His younger brother Michael (1825–1892) arrived in 1848 with a sister and their mother, Mary, who died that year.

How John Schiml occupied himself during his first years in Dayton is unknown. Michael apprenticed himself to a cooper, or barrel maker. But in 1851 or 1852, the two brothers started a brewery on Wayne Avenue at the corner of Hickory. (An 1893 *Dayton Daily Journal* reported the year was 1851, but Beers and Crew gave it as 1852.)

The original brewery was a two-story frame building, twenty-eight by fifty feet. What really distinguished it, though, was microscopic: the single-celled fungi of lager yeast. An unnamed cousin of the Schimls brought the first yeast stock from Boston, Beers wrote, and the brothers brewed Montgomery County's first batch of lager beer on December 13, 1852. They produced 1,200 barrels the next year. Lager beer had arrived.

The brewery stood just south of where U.S. 35 later split two neighborhoods that became national historic districts: Oregon to the north and South Park to the south. When the Schimls arrived, the whole area was budding with houses and shops. They operated as the Oregon Brewery from at least 1856, when *Williams' Dayton Directory for 1856–1857* listed it under that name, until the early 1870s, when directories started listing it as the Wayne Street Brewery.

John died in 1858 at age thirty-eight. Michael carried on the business, later joined by three sons: Aloysius C. (or Alois or Aloys), who clerked; John L., the bookkeeper; and Andrew M., the brewer and superintendent. The business prospered and grew on their watch. When a fire in July 1881 burned the stable and the roof of their icehouse, killing four horses and destroying three thousand bushels of malt, they replaced the whole plant with a bigger, three-story brewery and icehouse, both built of brick.

It was Michael's plan "to retire from active life in a short time, leaving the management of his brewery to his sons, who are thoroughly competent of

Location of Wayne Street Brewery. *From Combination Atlas Map of Montgomery County, Ohio (1875).*

imitating heir father's success in life," according to Beers. But it wasn't to be. John L. died in 1885 at age thirty-three, and Aloys died in 1891 at age twenty-seven. Only Andrew survived his father, dying in 1945 at age eighty-five. Aloys lived long enough to buy the brewery in 1889 with a brother-in-law, Frank J. Bucher, but land records show Michael kept the malting part of the business almost until his death in 1892 at age sixty-seven.

The Schimls' output of lager beer grew over the years. Michael turned out about 4,400 barrels yearly in the 1870s and '80s, according to Beers and Crew. Production seemed to falter in the wake of Aloys's and Michael's deaths, dropping to about 2,500 in the early 1890s, according to the April 24, 1893 *Dayton Daily Journal.* But it bounced back under Bucher's management, selling between 7,000 and 8,000 barrels in 1898, according to that year's *Brewer's Guide.* Bucher (1858–1936), a cigar maker who had married Michael's daughter, Susan, became sole proprietor, doing business as the Pioneer Brewery until 1900, when he sold it to another up-and-coming brewer, Louis L. Wehner.

The Schimls never dominated Dayton's brewing industry, but their lager beer transformed it. Henry Ferneding built his new brewery in 1859 expressly to produce lager, according to Beers. Ferneding kept the business going, taking on Lawrence Butz Jr. as a partner until 1864, when they sold the business to William Sander and John H. Stoppelmann. Jacob Stickle (1825–1908), another immigrant from Oldenburg, replaced Sander and became sole proprietor in 1868, producing only lager beer. The brewery did well enough that when fire damaged it in 1881—the same year Schiml's brewery burned—Stickle rebuilt it as a bigger brewery and was soon producing seven thousand barrels per year. He became one of Dayton's most prominent brewers.

Michael Schiml changed local brewing in another way when he took a young brewer under his wing who would dominate the industry in less than two decades.[7]

THE SCHWINDS

Among the most consequential figures in the Miami Valley's early brewing history were the Schwind brothers. Besides their brewing and business skills, their associations and marriages made the first ties that would bind Dayton's major brewing families into a virtual clan and establish a brewing industry twenty miles north in Troy.

The Schwinds (sometimes identified as "Schwint") emigrated in the late 1840s from Stadtprozelten, in northwestern Bavaria, where their father, Ignatz (or Ignatius), was a brewer. It's uncertain whether they traveled to America together, but once here, they sought their own fortunes in the brewing business.

The eldest Schwind, Joseph (circa 1818–1867), had a brewery going on South Main Street by 1850, according to census records. That year, he married another German transplant named Agnes Anastasia Wehner (1823–1885)—a name that would become prominent in Dayton brewing because of her future nephew, Louis Wehner (1866–1934). Titus Schwind (1820–1879), Joseph's younger brother by two years, settled in Troy, where census records show he was a brewer by 1849. The two youngest Schwinds, Coelestin (1825–1893) and Anton (1828–1862), worked in Titus's brewery in 1849 before joining Joseph in Dayton in 1850, according to the 1893 *Dayton Daily Journal* report.[8]

Joseph Schwind's Main Street Brewery stood on the west side of South Main Street between Franklin and Washington, about two blocks north of where Main bridged the canal. The brewery faced what was then the top of Warren Street, running southeast and likewise bridging the canal. As of this writing, South Patterson Boulevard traces the canal's path, and the brewery's place, at 411 South Main, is a vacant lot between a filling station and the Community Blood Center.

The *Journal* indicated Coelestin (or Cölestin or Celestin) worked at Joseph's brewery for a few years before taking a job that would change his life and the future of brewing in Dayton: he spent eleven months in the employment of Michael Schiml's lager beer brewery, where, the paper reported, Coelestin learned "valuable information" about the craft. The *Journal* added the two remained lifelong friends even as they became business rivals.

In 1854, Coelestin started his own business, the Canal Brewery. Anton (or Anthony) Schwind left Joseph's brewery to become Coelestin's partner. The Canal Brewery stood at 14 Logan Street, just two blocks northeast and across the canal from the Main Street Brewery. As of this writing, Logan is a nondescript brick street skirting the east side of a narrow park between East Sixth Street and Green; the park separates Logan from South Patterson Boulevard, but the few buildings along Logan have Patterson Boulevard addresses. The brewery is long gone.

Coelestin and Anton didn't immediately begin brewing lager beer. The *Journal* reported they only brewed "common beer" for several years until Coelestin built a much larger brewery in Dayton View. But Anton never saw it: he died in 1862 at age thirty-four.

Wayne Street Brewery, on the corner of Wayne Avenue and Hickory Street, after 1885. *Lutzenberger Collection, Dayton Metro Library.*

Despite being brothers in a foreign land, the three elder Schwinds seemed to want to live their own lives, independent of one another. One reason may have been religion. Coelestin's family attended Emmanuel Catholic Church, established in 1837 as a German territorial parish, and he rests at the church's Calvary Cemetery, just south of Carillon Historical Park. Titus was Lutheran, and Joseph and Anton may have been as well: all three were buried at Woodland, a community cemetery east of Brown Street. This division even extended to Joseph's widow, Agnes, and their children, who also rest at Calvary, two miles from Joseph.

Whatever their differences, the Schwinds kept strong family ties. For example, when Titus sold his Troy brewery in 1874—apparently in declining health, as he mentioned in his will—Coelestin's family took him in until his death in 1879. Coelestin hosted Titus's Lutheran funeral in his Dayton View mansion, with services officiated by the pastor of St. John's German Lutheran Church.

Dayton's First Woman Brewer

After Anton's death in 1862, his widow, Mary, carried on as co-owner of the property for a short time, but no evidence showing she managed the business was found. The first woman brewery proprietor of record was Agnes Wehner Schwind.

While Agnes and Joseph were wed in Dayton, census records indicate Agnes hailed from Joseph's native town of Stadtprozelten. If the Schwinds and Wehners weren't close in the old country, they became so in the new: in 1860, Joseph's household included Agnes; her mother, Mary A. Wehner; and Agnes's brother, Julius. Julius worked in the brewery in the 1860s before acquiring a saloon on South Jefferson Street, and he was the father of Louis Wehner, who would build his own Dayton brewery.

Joseph died in 1867. Agnes stayed with the brewery, whose address was the same as the family home. The 1870 census gives her occupation as "keeping house," but it also lists her as head of the household. It gives the title of "brewer" to their son William, eighteen, assisted by his brother Adolph, fourteen. But the business indexes of city directories list the brewery in Agnes's name from 1868 through 1882, except for the year 1875, when it lists Adolph as proprietor. Salem's book also identifies Agnes as a Dayton brewer.

The brewery did a modest business. Its output was the smallest by far of the four Dayton breweries in Salem's book. Even so, it made his list, with sales reported as 820 barrels in 1878. But Salem's figures also hinted at trouble. It reported Agnes's 1879 sales as 632 barrels—a drop of 22 percent from the preceding year. The sharp downturn contrasted with either modest gains or slight declines for Dayton's three biggest breweries—most tellingly, her brother-in-law's. Coelestin's new Dayton View Brewery, turning out the popular lager beer, topped Salem's list for Dayton with 6,150 barrels sold in 1878 and 5,977 in 1879, a dip of just 2 percent.

Coelestin's brewery was also becoming the family's economic center of gravity. A growing number of Schwinds found jobs there. Even Agnes's sons seemed to go back and forth, their residences switching from Agnes's home to Coelestin's and back again over the years. After 1882, the Main Street Brewery disappears from city directories, which simply list Agnes as a widow living at the brewery's address with her eldest son, William, and two daughters, Amelia and Magdalena (or Lena).

Michael Schiml's Wayne Street Brewery is gone, but this building across Hickory is one of several where Schimls lived. *Author's collection.*

The three Schwind children never married, and they stayed together even after Agnes's death. William eventually became a bookkeeper at his uncle Coelestin's brewery. Two days before Christmas 1907, the *Dayton Journal* carried a report about William's sudden collapse and death in a streetcar at age fifty-five. Full of lurid details, the report said nothing about a brewing background or his connection with one of Dayton's oldest breweries.

The newspaper was equally dismissive of Agnes Schwind's legacy. Sometime in the night on June 12, 1885, a heart attack took her as she slept. She was sixty-three. Her death rated a news story but apparently not a eulogy. "Found Dead in Her Bed," blurted the *Journal's* June 13 headline. The story was mainly about a servant girl's horror at finding her employer deceased. It made no mention of Agnes's groundbreaking career as a brewery proprietor.

Agnes Schwind may have been Dayton's first female brewery owner, but she wasn't the last. Another was her late husband's sister-in-law, Christina Schwind. More than inheriting a family business, Christina would become the first female president of an incorporated Dayton brewery.[9]

Schwind's Dayton View Brewery

Christina (or Christine) Latin (1835–1907) was born in Bavaria to Valentine and Barbara Hartman Latin. Her family came to the United States sometime in the 1840s and was living in Brookville, Indiana, by 1850, according to that year's census. Christina was the oldest of several siblings.

Census records hint growing up in the Latin household might have been challenging, or at least not typical of the times. Census sheets back then included a column to describe whether one was "deaf and dumb, blind, insane, idiotic, pauper, or convict." Another column was for describing one's occupation. In 1850, a census taker in Brookville wrote "crazy" on the line for Valentine Latin (circa 1817–1896). The space for his occupation was blank.

What did this mean? Was Valentine disabled by mental illness, leaving it to his wife and children to make ends meet? Was he a bit eccentric and between jobs when the census taker showed up? Or was he simply uncooperative and annoying that day? "Crazy" is hardly a clinical diagnosis, and this was six years before the birth of Sigmund Freud, the founder of psychoanalysis. Whatever the truth, something about Valentine must have been noteworthy:

while the 1870 census cited no disabilities, the 1880 census once again checked "insane" after his name. (Valentine wasn't found in 1860 census records for either Dayton or Brookville.)

Valentine's name first turned up in Ohio in *Williams' Dayton Directory for 1866–1867*, which listed him as a brewer in Coelestin's brewery. But at least some of his children had been in the state since the 1850s. Christina wed Coelestin in 1856. By 1860, her brother, Felix, then about nineteen, was working in Joseph Schwind's brewery. Her sister, Matilda, about fourteen, was boarding with Coelestin and Christina, where she also worked as a servant. Valentine may not have worked at the brewery very long, as city directories through 1895 sometimes list him as a cooper but often give no occupation. They place him on Burns Avenue and later on what was Monroe Avenue, both near Warren just a few blocks down from the brewery. He died in 1896.[10]

The Civil War claimed more than 600,000 lives and threatened to split the nation. Nobody escaped its effects, brewers included. The government needed money to pay for the conflict, so Congress passed the Internal Revenue Act of 1862. It taxed people and businesses widely, including beer drinkers, brewers and saloons. But the cost to Christina's family and Joseph's brewery was far more personal. In 1861, Felix enlisted in the Fifty-Eighth Regiment, Ohio Volunteer Infantry. His first battle came even before he left home: he fell ill with typhoid fever in January 1862. Not until February was he well enough to join his regiment, by then in Tennessee. What finally claimed Felix is unclear, but military records attest he didn't survive the war.[11]

Despite the conflict, Dayton continued to grow, and Coelestin Schwind's brewery prospered. In 1868, he began building a new brewery on the west bank of the Great Miami in Dayton View.

The new Dayton View Brewery was a sign of the city's galloping growth. Its population shot up by half in the 1860s, topping thirty thousand by the end of the decade. Dayton View was one of several small communities springing up across the Miami and Mad Rivers from Dayton. The year Schwind started building his brewery was the same year the city annexed Dayton View and several other plats in a general expansion that pushed its borders beyond the rivers. The next year, 1869, saw the formation of the city's first streetcar line, the Dayton Street Railroad Company. It ran horse-drawn streetcars east and west on Third Street. The Dayton View Street Railroad Company followed in 1871 to extend streetcar service out Salem Avenue.

Once named Logan, this unnamed street along South Patterson Boulevard was where Coelestin Schwind's Canal Brewery stood. *Author's collection.*

The two-story, brick brewery and malt house rose at what was then 212 River Street, later Riverview Terrace. It sprawled most of the way down to the river. It began operating in 1869 and turned out 1,400 barrels per year, according to Crew. By the late 1880s, the main brewery stood four stories high, with spires on each corner and a large cupola on top. The entire plant—including separate buildings for malting, ice-making and bottling— stretched 275 feet along River Street. An 1887 Sanborn insurance map shows the brewery with lagering cellars behind it and a wagon shed down near the river. It had seventeen workers. Yearly sales reached 14,000 barrels by 1887 and were on track to hit 22,000 in 1893, the *Dayton Daily Journal* reported. It had the capacity to turn out 60,000 barrels annually.

In the late 1890s, the city fire department built Fire House No. 9 next to the brewery's bottling plant. It appeared on the 1897 Sanborn insurance map. The two-story brick structure must have been a comfort to the workers: breweries had a nasty habit of catching fire, and Sanborn's map notes Schwind's still used lard-oil lamps in addition to modern gas lighting and gas-powered engines and boilers.[12]

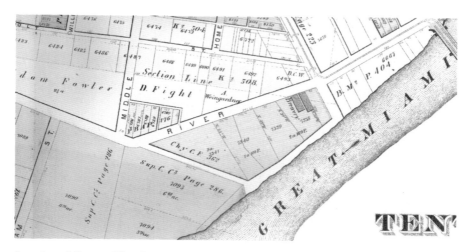

Location of Dayton View Brewery. *From* Combination Atlas Map of Montgomery County, Ohio *(1875)*.

Beer brought Coelestin real wealth. In 1874, he built a fourteen-room, Italianate brick mansion at 223 River, across from the brewery. A two-story, brick carriage house stood behind it. Schwind had practical reasons for such a large estate: he and Christina had eleven children, and city directories show a parade of family members moving in and out over the years.

In December 1892, Coelestin incorporated the brewery in Ohio as Schwind Brewing Company, "brewers and bottlers of export lager." Coelestin was president; Edmund J. (1859–1898), his eldest son, was vice-president; and Edward A. Hochwalt (1860–1935), husband of Coelestin's eldest daughter, Emma T., was secretary and treasurer.[13]

CHRISTINA SCHWIND, PRESIDENT

Coelestin died the next year, but neither Edmund nor Edward succeeded him. They both stayed in place. City directories listed no president until 1895, when *Williams' Dayton Directory for 1895–1896* listed Coelestin's widow, Christina, in the top position.

Christina was a captain of Dayton's brewing industry for about six years, and the Schwind business grew on her watch. Available numbers show sales grew about 32 percent, from twenty-five thousand barrels to thirty-three thousand, between 1895 and 1902. In June 1900, the *Dayton Daily News* reported the company, capitalized at $400,000 as an Ohio corporation, became a West Virginia company capitalized at $600,000.

The reorganization changed the name of the Schwind Brewing Company to the Schwind Brewery Company. It also replaced Christina with one of her sons, Michael Joseph. "Changes in the active management of the company have been made with a view to relieving Mrs. C. Schwind from the burden," the *News* reported on June 22.

By then in her sixty-sixth year, Christina may have felt ready to step down. She had set a solid record as the first woman president of an incorporated Dayton brewery. More important to her family, she had positioned both the company and the family for the future. In 1904, the Schwind Brewery Company merged with Dayton's other major beer companies to form the consolidated Dayton Breweries Company. And in March 1907, the Schwind family diversified its portfolio by forming the Schwind Realty Company, capitalized at $350,000. Christina's son Michael J. was principal incorporator.[14]

Christina Schwind wouldn't be the last woman brewer. A year after she stepped down, Anna Hollencamp would become president of the Hollencamp Ale Brewing Company. And Hollencamp Ale would include more than one woman executive. Women also ran breweries in Piqua, Sydney and Springfield. Their stories will come later.

Christina didn't live to see the realty company or, in 1912, the towering, eleven-story Schwind Building that rose on South Ludlow Street between Third and Fourth. She was one of three Schwinds who died in 1907. Two of her sons, Michael and William, died in December at ages thirty-three and fifty-five, respectively. Michael succumbed to Bright's disease, an old term for an affliction of the kidneys. The *Dayton Daily Journal* eulogized him in a 250-word story recognizing him as president of Schwind Realty and a director of Dayton Breweries. William, as previously noted, drew melodramatic coverage for his fatal collapse in a streetcar.

But of Christina, who died on January 17 at age seventy-one, only a forty-four-word death notice appeared in the *Dayton Daily Journal*. It identified her as Coelestin's widow.[15]

A Monument to Beer

The Schwind brewery stood until Prohibition. But the family's legacy lived on in Coelestin Schwind's Dayton View mansion and the realty company's

Schwind Building. The Schwinds eventually vacated the home, and their realty company leased it out. In the 1920s, the sisters Josephine and Hermene Schwarz moved in. On the first floor, they set up their Schwarz School of Dance, which meshed classical ballet with modern moves and made them renowned pioneers of the art. In 1937, they formed the Experimental Group for Young Dancers, forerunner of the Dayton Ballet.

Across the street, internationally known photographer Jane Reece bought the old fire station in 1924 and converted it into her home and studio. The Schwind house was converted to apartments and torn down in 1963. As of this writing, Reece's home still stands as an apartment building, and the brewery site next to it is a small park named in her memory.

The downtown Schwind Building was faced in white terra cotta and finished throughout with mahogany and marble, as the realty company described it in a full-page ad in the December 14, 1913 *Dayton Daily News*. The tower joined a classy new commercial district on South Ludlow—"Dayton's 'Fifth Avenue,'" the ad dubbed it. One neighbor was the Dayton Daily News Building, just erected at the northwest corner of Fourth and Ludlow by publisher and future Ohio governor James M. Cox. Its Corinthian columns made it look more like a bank than a newspaper. Across Ludlow stood the ten-year-old Dayton Arcade, a block of connected buildings with a glass rotunda in the middle.

The swanky district eventually declined. The Arcade closed in 1990, and the Cox Media Group vacated the newspaper building in 2007. A demolition crew dynamited the Schwind Building in 2013. The site remains vacant as of this writing. But in its day, it was a monument not only to the Schwinds but also to the potential of Annie Wittenmyer's "rough class of foreigner" to become a leader in commercial development by harnessing the economic power of beer.[16]

This apartment building on Riverview Terrace was once Dayton Fire House No. 9, built next to the Dayton View Brewery. *Author's collection.*

36

CHAPTER 2

DAYTON BREWERIES

THE GRAND CONSOLIDATION

A few years after the Schwinds came to Dayton, another German band of brothers arrived. Michael, Adam, Frederick, John and George Schantz spent their childhoods in Hesse-Darmstadt (now Darmstadt, a city south of Frankfurt in the southwestern German state of Hessen). In 1855, they all immigrated to the United States except George, then about four; he came later.

Most of what's published about the Schantz brothers is focused on Adam (1839–1903), a penniless immigrant who would reach the millionaires' ranks, and his son Adam Jr. (1867–1921), who would become one of Dayton's most influential business leaders. The consolidation of most of Dayton's breweries and saloons was only a part of the legacy they would leave.

The elder Adam Schantz was a "poor young man of fifteen years" when he emigrated, according to his obituary in the *Dayton Daily News*. It said his first stop was in Altoona, Pennsylvania, where an uncle already lived and ran a flour mill. It didn't name the uncle, but the 1860 census for Altoona listed a miller from Hesse-Darmstadt named Michael Schantz. An obituary in the *American Brewers' Review* also identified the uncle as Michael.

Adam worked at the mill for about a year before coming to Dayton, where he learned butchering from another Hesse-Darmstadt transplant, Michael Olt (1829–1894). Olt lived in the Dayton View area, then a part of Madison Township.

How Schantz found Olt isn't clear. Census records of the time show Michael's was one of several Olt families then in the region. But having

Adam Schantz Sr. was larger than life—and still is in this sculpture at Woodland Cemetery. *Author's collection.*

a common hometown, as with the Schwinds and Wehners, suggests the families knew each other back in Germany. Michael Olt's mentoring of young Adam was just the beginning of a relationship that would intertwine the Olts and Schantzes in Dayton.

Another step toward creating a clan of Dayton's major brewing families came in 1863, when Adam wed Mary Salome (or Saloma) Latin (1844–1927), one of Christina Schwind's sisters. Their union also connected the Schantz family to the Wehners through Christina's brother-in-law, Joseph Schwind, who was married to Agnes Wehner. Adam's brother George (1851–1917), who may have known the Schwinds through Christina, started his career in the Schwind brewery. And in 1870, the Olts married into the clan with the wedding of Adam's younger brother Frederick Schantz (1844–1931) to Barbara Olt (1845–1923), an apparent sister of Michael Olt. The bonds would grow and strengthen over the years.[17]

From Ocean to Riverside

All of this followed Adam's arrival in Dayton—and his prompt departure. The young man seemed smitten by wanderlust. According to his obituary in the May 20, 1903 *American Brewers' Review*, he stayed in Dayton only until he had saved enough money to make his way to Chicago, where he tried his hand in the Windy City's big meatpacking plants. After a year, he moved on to St. Louis and then returned to Dayton in the fall of 1858. The next year, unable to stay put, he traveled to New Orleans and hired on with a meat supplier to ocean steamers. There, a ship's captain granted him passage to England in trade for work. Somehow on the voyage, he fell overboard. His story would have ended in the cold Atlantic but for alert crewmen who plucked him from the waves with grappling hooks.

Schantz survived to reach England and return to his hometown in Germany, but soon he was on the move again—to Frankfurt, then Hamburg and then back to England, where he arrived in London with nothing to his name but half a loaf of pumpernickel. He managed to find work, and by the summer of 1862 he had saved enough to return to Dayton, where he settled down for a career in the meat business. He opened a shop downtown, married and bought a homestead on Covington Pike (now North Main Street).

About 1871, he moved to Dayton View, where he built a home on River (now West Riverview) near Central, across Salem from Coelestin and Christina Schwind. He built a slaughterhouse along the river to supply his downtown meat markets.

City directories show Adam's brother Frederick also operated a meat market downtown, and later their brothers John and Michael opened a family grocery and feed business near Adam's shop.

Their youngest brother, George (1851–1917), was the last Schantz on the scene but the first to brew. Records disagree about when he arrived from Germany. The 1900 census gives 1858, when he was about seven, which begs the question of who brought him. The 1910 census gives 1872, which conflicts with other records that show him here earlier. The 1893 feature in the *Dayton Daily News* gives 1867, the same year he hired on as a cellar hand at Coelestin's brewery at about age sixteen for eighteen dollars per month. This is consistent with the 1870 census, which has George living and working in the brewery. He quit that year to leave Dayton for Milwaukee, where he joined the huge Phillip Best Brewing Company (later Pabst). After a stint there, he worked at breweries in Chicago, St. Louis and Cleveland—no doubt soaking up knowledge about how big-city breweries worked—before returning to Dayton in 1873 to become Coelestin's foreman.

About nine years later, in 1882, George bought Adam's slaughterhouse and converted it into the Riverside Brewery, with Adam as his partner. Adam's son Adam Jr. (1867–1921), the second of an eventual thirteen siblings, joined the enterprise as bookkeeper after having worked in his father's meat business. He was no older than fifteen at the time.

It's unknown how Coelestin reacted to this new brewery rising along the river within sight of his own, erected by his former foreman and the husband of his wife's sister. It produced seven thousand barrels its first year, according to Crew's *History of Dayton, Ohio*. This was less than half of the fifteen thousand barrels the Dayton View Brewery turned out the same year, but it was a strong start. By the end of 1888, the Riverside Brewery had grown to seven buildings, and it was pushing ahead in sales—eighteen thousand barrels compared to Schwind's fourteen thousand in the preceding year.

On the other hand, both breweries were growing, and the self-proclaimed Gem City's population was soaring: after ballooning by half in the 1860s, it had swelled by nearly 27 percent in the 1870s and by more than half again

Riverside Brewery sometime before 1919. *Miami Conservancy District.*

in the 1880s. Coelestin might have figured Dayton had more demand for beer than one brewery could meet. Why leave the rest to others? The two breweries weren't alone in the market. Besides, another brewery five hundred feet upstream from his home had to be better than a slaughterhouse.

However Coelestin took it, records show no sign it opened a rift between the families. Just the opposite: in 1887, George sold his interest in the brewery to his brother Adam and teamed up on a new venture with Louis A. Schwind (1854–1895). Louis was a son of the late Anton Schwind, but he must have been like a son to Coelestin, who had become his guardian after Anton's death in 1862. Louis had worked in the brewery since age sixteen, a few years after George had started there.

Their venture? Yet another beer start-up, the Gem City Brewery, also known as Schantz & Schwind.[18]

Schantz and Schwind Team Up

George and Louis built their brewery on Perry Street south of Byard (later Auto Club Drive), a site later occupied by the Greater Dayton Regional Transit Authority's offices and bus barn. Daytonians did, indeed, seem able to consume all the beer they could brew. As the Dayton View and Riverside breweries grew, so did Gem City—built with a thirty-thousand-barrel capacity, it produced six thousand barrels in 1888 and twelve thousand in 1890. It added a bottling plant in 1893, and in 1894, it was incorporated as the Schantz & Schwind Brewing Company, capitalized at $250,000. Sales continued to grow, according to reports in the annual *Brewer's Guide*.

Over time, George Schantz would expand his business résumé as a director of First Savings and Banking, Dayton Iron and Steel and Dayton Street Railway. He was married to Emma Knecht and then, after her death in 1890, to Tilla Rehfus.

Nearly from the start, Schantz & Schwind also included a Wehner. Louis L. Wehner (1866–1934) was the son of Julius Wehner and a nephew of Agnes Wehner Schwind, Anton's widow. A.W. Drury wrote in his *History of the City of Dayton and Montgomery County* that Louis attended school until age sixteen, when he "put aside his text books and learned the carpenter's trade, which he followed for three years." But city directories show him working in his father's saloon until 1888, when they found him keeping the books at Schantz & Schwind, the same year he married Clara E. Linneman.

Ties between the Olt and Schantz families continued to grow. In 1893, Frederick "Fred" Olt (1874–1958), a son of John Olt and apparent nephew of Barbara Olt Schantz, was hired on at the Riverside Brewery as an assistant bookkeeper. Half a century earlier, Fred's apparent uncle Michael Olt had taught Adam Schantz the meat business. The ties grew again on New Year's Day 1901, when Adam Schantz Jr. married Mary Eva Olt (1872–1952), Fred's sister.

Until Fred Olt started working at the Riverside Brewery, the Olts had been connected to the brewing scene only by marriage. Another brewing tie followed in 1895 with the passing of Louis Schwind, co-founder of Schantz & Schwind. His death opened the secretary's seat for Louis Wehner. Taking Wehner's old job as bookkeeper was Charles J. Olt (1866–1940), brother of Fred and Mary. This put four Olts firmly in the Schantz and Schwind orbit: the three Olt siblings and their apparent aunt, Frederick Schantz's wife, Barbara. These extensive business and family ties gave no hints of the breakaway venture the Olt brothers would launch.[19]

Half a mile east of the Gem City Brewery, Michael Schiml's old plant was still open as the Pioneer Brewery, owned since 1889 by Frank J. Bucher. At the turn of the century, Bucher decided to focus on his cigar-making business. Louis Wehner bought the brewery on August 20, 1900, but soon closed it.

Similarly, in 1901 Wehner bought and then shuttered the Third Street Brewery. It had stood at 1513 East Third since at least 1854, when a Baden emigrant, Joseph Straub (1829–1909), had begun brewing there. Straub's obituary reported he built the two-story brick brewery, but other accounts state he bought it from an unnamed earlier brewer. City directories indicate he only owned it briefly, while Frederick Euchenhofer had brewed there from the 1860s nearly until his death in 1891, except during his service in the Civil War. Peter J. Altherr ran it for a short time until Wehner closed it forever.

Just what Wehner planned for the two breweries isn't clear, but he was soon involved in a much bigger venture: Edward Pape Sr., president of the Teutonia Fire Insurance Company and vice-president of Teutonia National Bank, incorporated the Wehner Brewing Company with J.H. Finke as vice-president. Louis Wehner joined as secretary-treasurer, with his wife, Clara, and a J. Schumacher as additional incorporators. They capitalized the company at $100,000.[20]

Wehner Brewing ordered a whole new plant with a capacity of thirty thousand barrels per year. It was soon rising west of the Great Miami

James Ritty's Pony House was a prominent Dayton saloon in the late 1880s. *Lutzenberger Collection, Dayton Metro Library.*

River at the northeast corner of Concord and Scoville Streets, according to *Williams' Dayton Directory for 1900–1901*. It was in the up-and-coming Edgemont neighborhood. Its place on modern maps would have been south of Albany Street between Hopeland and Edwin C. Moses Boulevard. The brewery was a five-story structure of brick and steel. It made headlines as it was going up late in 1901—especially when the rush to finish it put two workers' lives in peril.

Wehner's Brewery and the Pit of Death

The brewery was to be up and running by spring. But the plant included massive grain bins, eight feet across and seventy feet tall, either made of or lined with slow-drying cement. To save time, Wehner ordered his chief engineer, Tony Herberger, to set charcoal furnaces inside the bins to warm the walls. On the morning of December 4, 1901, Herberger and another worker, Edward Harmon, lowered the furnaces into the bins from manholes at the top. As reported in the next day's *Dayton Daily News*, the furnaces burned steadily until mid-afternoon, when Herberger climbed down a ladder to refuel them. Watching from the manhole, Harmon quickly grew alarmed as Herberger's lamp sputtered out and the bin fell dark and eerily silent.

Wehner and Henry Nordhouse, a millwright from Chicago, were installing equipment on the third floor when Harmon ran to them in a panic. They raced back to the manhole. Harmon volunteered to go down on a rope to fetch Herberger, but Nordhouse—younger, lighter and more athletic—insisted he go instead. He tied a rope around his waist and held a second one for Herberger. The unnamed reporter described what he imagined as Nordhouse's brave descent "with a smile of utter fearlessness on his lips."

The bin engulfed Nordhouse in what the reporter called "terrible fumes" and a "sickening smell." But the greatest danger was odorless: carbon monoxide gas, a deadly combustion byproduct. Nordhouse's lamp died, but

Frederick Euchenhofer Brewery or Third Street Brewery. *Lutzenberger Collection, Dayton Metro Library.*

he found Herberger's motionless form and managed to tie the second rope around him. Then he, too, collapsed.

When Nordhouse's rope went limp, the men at the top hauled him up. As the reporter wrote with melodramatic flair, "They pulled him to the manhole, and as he was dragged away from the breath of death, he sputtered between closed teeth, 'I've got him, pull.'"

Herberger was unresponsive as they brought him up and laid him on the floor, but a medical doctor named C.T. Shepherd arrived and administered a bucket of water to his face. Herberger gradually revived, and the others took him to his home across the street to recover.

The brewery started up in early 1902 and began turning out lager beer and ale. One year after the accident, the newspaper reported Wehner Brewing already needed to expand.[21]

COMPETITION

By scrapping the Pioneer and Third Street breweries, Wehner had eliminated two old plants with no family connections. But other competitors abounded at the turn of the twentieth century.

Jacob Stickle's City Brewery

The City Brewery (not the Gem City Brewery of Schantz and Schwind) could trace its roots all the way back to 1843, when Henry Ferneding had opened his first brewery on Kenton Street. He had relocated the business to a new brewery on Brown Street just south of Apple. It had gone through a succession of owners until Jacob Stickle (1825–1908) became sole proprietor in 1868. Another immigrant from Württemberg, Stickle came to Dayton by way of New Orleans in 1849. He worked as a butcher and had his own market stall until he bought the brewery. He was married to Barbara Drecksel in 1851. "No beer brewed is purer, more delicious or healthful" than Stickle's "pure old lager," his newspaper ads boasted. Stickle died in 1908 at age eighty-three. But at the turn of the century, he was still brewing beer.[22]

Jacob Stickle's City Brewery, in about 1875. *From* Combination Atlas Map of Montgomery County, Ohio *(1875).*

Dayton Ale Brewery and Theodore Hollenkamp

The Dayton Ale Brewery had been around under various names since the mid-1850s, when three German immigrants—August Becherer, Henry Hilgefort and John B. Wager—started it at the southeast corner of Hickory and Brown Streets. City directories show Hilgefort (1828–1913) and Wager (1827–1899) left after a few years, while Becherer (1826–1885) stayed with the brewery. He picked up a partner named Henry Hussman for several years in the 1860s, when the business became known as the Ohio Brewery. In 1864, the Ohio Infantry called him for Civil War duty, but he was soon released and went back to brewing. His son, Frank, later joined him as a partner. Land records indicate Becherer lost the brewery in a sheriff's sale in 1878, about the same time he opened a small brewery and beer garden on Brown Street in Oakwood. It last appeared as a saloon in *Williams' Dayton City Directory for 1883–1884*, two years before Becherer died.

Theodore Hollenkamp (1834–1901) bought the old Ohio Brewery in 1885 with John F. Oehlschlager as a partner, according to a biographical sketch in Frank Conover's *Centennial Portrait and Biographical Record of the City of Dayton*. They reopened it as the Dayton Ale Brewery. Oehlschlager left after two years, replaced by Henry Kramer. Kramer sold his interest in 1895, leaving Hollenkamp as sole owner.

Theodore Hollenkamp was a nephew of Bernard Hollencamp, who had been Henry Ferneding's partner in the City Brewery before buying his own in Xenia. (Published reports often spelled Theodore's last name with a "c," but his company later made "Hollenkamp" its distinctive brand name, and Calvary Cemetery uses this spelling for Theodore and other family members.) Born in Hanover, Theodore had immigrated to America and worked

The Hollencamp brewery at Hickory and Brown went by several names from the 1850s to the 1900s. *Karla Hollencamp Collection.*

in Cincinnati breweries for some time before joining his uncle in Xenia. Bernard died in 1872, but his sons continued to operate it as Hollencamp Brothers, and *Wiggins & McKillop's Directory of Greene County for 1878* listed Theodore as an employee. He remained in Xenia long enough for one of his sons, Theodore D. (1882–1935), to be born in Xenia in 1882, but by 1885 he was in Dayton. He proved a match for his cousins: Dayton Ale and the Xenia brewery each sold between three and four thousand barrels in 1898, according to that year's *Brewer's Guide.*

Theodore Sr. died in June 1901. His family carried on, incorporating in November as the Hollencamp Ale Brewing Company. Beer history buffs might remember Hollenkamp as one of the few breweries to survive Prohibition, but it also deserves recognition as the only Dayton brewery run almost entirely by women.

The Hollenkamp Women

Theodore D.'s obituary reported he became head of the company upon his father's death, but city directories list Theodore's widow, Anna (1843–1907), as president from 1901 until her death in 1907. Theodore D., about nineteen when his father died, worked as superintendent until he succeeded his mother. He guided the company through Prohibition, renaming and refitting it in 1919 to sell soft drinks as Hollenkamp Products. But supporting him were four Hollenkamp women who ran the company themselves after his death.

Besides Anna, Hollenkamp women in top seats included Theodore D.'s elder sister Elizabeth M. (1874–1965), who became secretary-treasurer in 1901. Anna L. (1871–1957), the eldest Hollenkamp sibling, became vice-president in about 1919 and then president after Theodore D.'s death in 1935. Also stepping up were their sister Helene in 1934, who served as treasurer and then vice-president, and his widow, Louise A. (Bucher) (1884–1966), also as a vice-president. They served until at least 1940, according to city directories—a span of about forty years for Elizabeth and about twenty-one years for Anna L. Some men held senior positions over the years, but women occupied most of the officers' seats. As with Agnes Wehner Schwind and Christina Latin Schwind, the Hollenkamp women went essentially unrecognized as brewing company executives during their lifetimes, and they remain so as of this writing.[23]

Nick Thomas and the Hydraulic Brewery

In the first half of the nineteenth century, industry in the Miami Valley depended on its rivers for power. Low dams and hydraulic canals tapped the streams' energy to drive mill wheels and factory turbines. In the 1840s, the Dayton Hydraulic Company dug a trench for the Upper Hydraulic from the Mad River northeast of the city into downtown, where it emptied into the canal. Numerous mills and factories rose along its course. One was an old sawmill that John B. Wager converted into a brewery shortly after he left Becherer. He called it the Hydraulic Brewery, a drab if fitting name. City directories placed it at the southwest corner of East First and North Beckel streets. As of this writing, it's an industrial lot.

Nicholas "Nick" Thomas. *From Memoirs of the Miami Valley, vol. 3.*

Land records show Wager lost the brewery in 1870, and Henry Ferneding and his son Clement bought it in a sheriff's auction. They owned the property briefly, while two partners named Nicholas Metz and Anthony Braun ran the business. The brewery's legacy would lie in the rags-to-riches story of a German farmhand who walked into town penniless in 1848.

Nicholas "Nick" Thomas (1825–1913) was born in Esterwegen, a municipality then in the kingdom of Hanover, later in Lower Saxony in northwestern Germany. Drury's biographical sketch describes him as the son of a sheep farmer who died when Nicholas was fourteen. He stayed on the farm, but not necessarily by choice. Drury wrote Hanover's army prevented Thomas from leaving the kingdom, apparently to keep able-bodied men handy for military duty. Drury wrote Thomas gained his release at about age twenty-one when he failed a medical exam. If true, it begs the question of whether Thomas persuaded, tricked or bribed his examiner, as in America he proved to be one of the hardest-working immigrants ever to tend a brew kettle.

Emigrating in late 1847, Thomas landed in New Orleans and continued by boat up the Mississippi and Ohio Rivers to Cincinnati. In the middle of January 1848, despite severe cold, he walked to Dayton in stocking feet—carrying his boots in a pack, Drury wrote. Why the boots were on his back instead of his feet Drury didn't explain; Thomas might have thought them too precious for mere walking, or they might have been new and so stiff they caused blisters.

Thomas found work cleaning the canal, but his destination was an uncle's farm at Decatur, Indiana. After two weeks in Dayton, Thomas completed his trek, still afoot. Drury didn't describe his route from Dayton, but the straight-line distance to Decatur is about eighty-four miles. Thomas spent the winter hauling wood from his uncle's farm to a soap factory, and then he took a job on a canalboat transporting stone from Huntington to Fort Wayne. He fell ill with ague—an archaic term for malarial fevers and aches that plagued canal workers—but nine months later, he returned to Dayton. He walked from Decatur to Minster in Auglaize County before finishing the journey on a canalboat.[24]

Thomas continued to make his living with hard labor. No description of his size was found, but a newspaper report years later suggested he was a big man, carrying 230 pounds in a "splendid physique." He worked in the Dickey stone quarry for three years and then held a variety of hard jobs, including driver of a four-horse team hauling logs to the Longstead sawmill—the same mill Wager later turned into a brewery.

Thomas gradually advanced to less menial jobs. In 1857, he bought his own horse and wagon for a drayage, or freight service, and in 1871 he took a job as night watchman in banks. He saved up enough money to open a grocery store and saloon on the corner of East Third and Front Streets, and in 1880 or 1881—accounts differ—he launched a new career as proprietor of the Hydraulic Brewery. He was in his mid-fifties by then.

Thomas started with a partner named George A. Weddle. They owned the brewery and other property together until 1892, when they ended their partnership. Weddle moved to Xenia and became associated with the Hollencamp brewery there. Thomas sold the brewery in 1906, but he remained with it to the end of his life. He worked in his office regularly until his last few days, according to his obituary in the August 23, 1913 *Dayton Daily Journal*. It reported he died "one of the wealthiest men" in town and had become known as "the youngest old man in the city."

Back at the turn of the century, Thomas was still building his business. In 1900, Drury reported the Hydraulic Brewery's output as eleven thousand barrels, more than an order of magnitude greater than the six hundred barrels of his first year. But like Wehner across town, Thomas saw the potential for more. In October 1901, the *Dayton Daily News*

An undated view of the canal, looking north, with the Sachs-Pruden building at right.
Lutzenberger Collection, Dayton Metro Library.

reported he was adding a six-story, $75,000 brewhouse that would bring his plant's capacity to seventy thousand barrels. In June 1900, according to the directory of incorporated companies in *Williams' Dayton Directory for 1901–1902*, he incorporated his business as the N. Thomas Brewing Company, and with it he created a tie to the Schantz-Schwind clan: the company's secretary was Edward Hochwalt, husband of the late Coelestin Schwind's eldest daughter, Emma T., and a former secretary-treasurer of Schwind Brewing.[25]

Sachs-Pruden

Beer hasn't been made there in a century, but the Sachs-Pruden Ale Company's brewhouse survives as Dayton's only original example of nineteenth-century brewery architecture. The four-story brick building stands downtown between South Patterson Boulevard on the west and Wyandot Street on the east, halfway between Fourth and Fifth Streets. As of

Sachs and Pruden's first business partnership, about 1875. *From* Combination Atlas Map of Montgomery County, Ohio *(1875)*.

this writing, it houses the administrative offices of the Dayton Metro Library, and for many years prior it was the home of Hauer Music. But its long, western wall once faced the Miami and Erie Canal. The roots of its business were in ale, but of a different kind: ginger ale.

Edward Sachs (1851–1901) was a first-generation Daytonian, the son of immigrants from Baden. He worked as a clerk near his family's home at 219 East Second Street, near St. Clair, until he teamed up in 1874 with another Dayton native.

David Pruden (1855–1910) was a son of Alfred Pruden, a successful Dayton real estate investor who built the Pruden Block building on the southeast corner of Fifth and Main Streets (now the site of the Dayton Convention Center). Alfred bought his eldest sons, Alfred Jr. and Henry B., one thousand acres of land in southern Kansas for a cattle ranch, according to a biographical sketch in J. Fletcher Brennan's *A Biographical Cyclopædia*. Such largess to his sons suggests he might well have helped nineteen-year-old David start his first venture with Edward when they opened a store on the southeast corner of East Third and St. Clair. *Williams' Dayton City Directory for 1875–1876* billed them as "Dealers in Drugs, Medicine, Chemicals, Paints, Oils &c [et cetera]."

Edward's father, Adam, was a varnisher, which might have influenced Edward's interest in chemistry. He gravitated toward drugs and medicinal products, especially extracts used to make what were believed to be health-promoting beverages. Zeroing in on ginger root, he developed a brand of ginger ale extract that quickly built a name for Sachs & Pruden. The company sold it to bottlers nationwide, along with a tonic it dubbed "A.T. 8 Agaric," said to be just the thing for dyspepsia. Advertisements and postcards featured images of colorfully dressed women, sometimes bare-breasted—to convince customers of the healthful nature of their products, no doubt.

In 1883, Sachs and Pruden brought on board Pruden's elder brother, Henry B., who evidently had returned from Kansas. A year later, they relocated to Fourth and Wyandot, where they bottled as well as brewed. "The firm was wonderfully successful for a number of years," the *Dayton Daily News* reported in 1901.

As long as they were brewing ginger ale, why not make the hard kind? Dayton couldn't seem to get enough beer. In 1888, the group formed the Sachs-Pruden Ale Company, with Edward Sachs as president, David Pruden as vice-president and Henry B. as secretary-treasurer, as well as other investors. Apparently certain of huge demand and flush with $500,000 in capital stock, they commissioned a big new brewery, including a malt house and ice plant. The building they already occupied became the bottling plant.

But Sachs and Pruden were limiting their line to old-fashioned ales and porters at a time when lager beer was sweeping the country. "This plan was not successful," the *Dayton Daily News* reported, so in 1891 they split up the company. The Sachs-Pruden Brewing Company dropped "Ale" from its name and gave lager beer top billing. David Pruden was its president. Sachs formed the Sachs-Pruden Manufacturing Company, soon renamed the Sachs-Pruden Ginger Ale Company, with Charles E. Thomas as president

A SET OF 10 OF THESE PHOTOS. SENT FOR 10·2¢ STAMPS BY ADDRESSING. SACHS-PRUDEN & CO. DAYTON, O.

❋ SACHS-PRUDENS "A.T. 8." AGARIC. ❋
· THE GREAT TONIC AND STIMULANT ·

Sachs-Pruden's "A.T.8. Agaric" ads, like this one from Adam Becker's collection, featured alluring and sometimes bare-breasted women. *Author's collection.*

A Sachs-Pruden Brewing Company bottle collected by Adam Becker. *Author's collection.*

and himself as vice-president. It produced ginger ale in a plant at First and Foundry.

On April 24, 1893, the *Dayton Daily Journal* praised "the phenomenal growth" of Sachs-Pruden's lager beer sales, which "surpasses, we understand, that of any brewery in Dayton." In a nearly full-page collection of brewers' profiles headlined "Dayton Beer Barons," the *Journal* claimed Sachs-Pruden brewed more than eighteen thousand barrels between 1891 and 1892 and prophesied "a most brilliant future" for it.

But the feature read as if the brewers themselves wrote the profiles. Every brewer, it seemed, was among the best in town and on his way to the top. In reality, Sachs-Pruden was sinking. David Pruden was gone by 1894. It fell into receivership, reemerging in 1895 as the Dayton Brewing Company. Heading it was Charles Whealen, president of the Dayton Ice Manufacturing and Cold Storage Company.

Pruden was only about thirty-nine when he left the company, but later census reports listed him as retired. In 1910, he died of heart failure at age fifty-four. Edward Sachs continued with his ginger ale business, even working on weekends, until Saturday, January 14, 1899. That afternoon, he was in his office when he suffered an apparent stroke. "For the past several weeks he has been in ill health," the *Dayton Daily News* reported. "Saturday morning he complained somewhat of his condition, and while going through his regular duties he was seized with an attack, which affected his right side. He was taken to his home in a carriage." Sachs apparently remained paralyzed until his death two years later. He was fifty.[26]

National Competition and Temperance

Such was the landscape of Dayton's brewing industry around the turn of the twentieth century. But outside forces threatened to change it. In the late 1800s, big-city brewers were beginning to harness new technology—pasteurization, refrigeration and railroads—to reach beyond their local markets. As the century rolled over, big brands such as Milwaukee's Joseph Schlitz Brewing Company and Budweiser of St. Louis were popping up locally, competing for sales.

Dayton's biggest brewers weren't oblivious to the threat. Adam Schantz spelled it out in a December 3, 1900 letter to Sereno E. Payne, a Republican congressman of Auburn, New York, who chaired the House Ways and Means Committee. At the time, the brewing industry was urging Congress to lower the federal tax on beer—dubbed the "war tax" because it had been made law to help pay for the Civil War and boosted again in 1898 for the Spanish-American War. Some brewers argued the tax would force small companies out of business and leave consumers at the mercy of a few major ones. But in his letter to Payne, republished in the *Dayton Daily News*, Schantz argued the opposite was true:

> [T]*he smaller brewers, of which I am one, never feared the war tax half as much as the unfair competitors. It is more the fault of the big brewers, who for years have forced their beer into the neighborhoods of their smaller competitors at such ruinous prices and methods that the smaller competitors were unable to compete. Those big brewers have for years bought real estate in the cities before the very eyes of the smaller and weaker competitors at 100 percent more than the actual value of the properties, boasting of their rich concerns, and the millions behind them. Now they see how unwisely they have acted; not one half of their properties bring them a percentage, and this war tax and other expenses make them howl.*[27]

If Schantz's angst had a name, it might have been the Schlitz Palm Garden—not the opulent entertainment hall of the Schlitz Hotel in Milwaukee, but one with the same name in downtown Dayton. Opened in 1896, the original featured a large, vaulted space filled with potted palms and tables on a deep-red carpet, reflecting the German tradition of tree-shaded beer gardens. In 1900, the *Dayton Daily News* reported another was planned at 213–217 South Jefferson Street, just south of Fifth. Its proprietor was Paul Wohlbruck, a Schlitz representative from Milwaukee. What he opened in 1901 was no less than "one of the most charming places to lounge imaginable," according to a profile in the 1902 *Dayton Daily News*. "The first floor is refreshingly arranged with 25 or 30 magnificent palms" and featured an orchestra, it reported. Its amenities included second-floor rooms that staged vaudeville acts, a third-floor ballroom and a rooftop garden.

The saloon in Paul Wohlbruck's Schlitz Palm Garden. *Detroit Publishing Company Photograph Collection, Library of Congress.*

Wohlbruck's Schlitz Palm Garden didn't last, and it isn't clear how close it came to matching the newspaper's description, much less its Milwaukee namesake. Research turned up no pictures of it, but the Library of Congress preserves a photo of an associated saloon. It depicts a narrow, drab room bisected by a long, plain bar and foot rail. Behind the bar, halfway down, hangs a sign prominently advertising Schlitz beer. After 1902, word of it and Wohlbruck disappeared from Dayton publications. (Wohlbruck may have moved to Toledo, where the 1904 city directory listed a man with the same name as a Pabst Brewing manager.)

The Palm Garden's quick demise might have been one reason why a December 20 *Dayton Daily News* article boasted Dayton's beer was so good that no outside brewer stood a chance in the local market. "Fine quality is the wall" that would allow "no foreign opposition in the city," it asserted. The article covered half a page, and it once again read as if the brewers themselves had penned it. But the Palm Garden made it clear the enemy wasn't simply at the gate—it was already downtown, putting Big Beer brands in local saloons.

Another threat was the growing movement to reduce or eliminate the selling of alcoholic beverages. Ohio beer makers had a front-row seat to the temperance movement. Schantz couldn't have missed the formation of the Woman's Christian Temperance Union in Cleveland in 1874 or the rise of the Anti-Saloon League, organized in Oberlin in 1893. Both became powerful forces in the Prohibition movement. A nationwide ban might have seemed unlikely at the turn of the century, but the temperance movement was working relentlessly to restrict or ban alcohol at the state and local levels. In March 1900, the Ohio Senate narrowly defeated the Clark "local option" bill, which would have allowed voters to make cities and wards go dry.

All of these factors—local rivals, national brands and the temperance movement—might have figured in what happened next to Dayton's brewing industry. Another, without a doubt, was the death of Adam Schantz.[28]

CIRCLING THE (BEER) WAGONS

Like Coelestin Schwind before him but in even greater measure, Adam Schantz Sr. showed how America made it possible for a poor German immigrant to work his way to wealth and drive economic growth in his community. Leveraging his meat business and then his brewery, Schantz amassed a fortune in real estate and other interests. He bought a large plat in Oakwood and began the development of a garden-like neighborhood that his son, Adam Jr. (1867–1921), finished as Schantz Park—later a National Historic District—that included Adam Jr.'s own palatial home at 202 East Schantz Avenue. Schantz Sr. also bought a vacation home in Daytona, Florida, where he died in April 1903. He was sixty-four.

As with the Schantz Park project, the younger Adam carried on his father's interests—especially the brewery, where he had been developing his business skills since age fifteen. Steeped in his father's ways but younger and full of drive, he became the new Adam Schantz. Few published reports ever labeled him "Jr."

Almost immediately, a major business venture by outsiders put Schantz to the test. In 1903, while Dayton's Wright brothers were away in North Carolina, quietly changing history with their airplane, investors from Cleveland and Hamilton just as quietly optioned Dayton's major breweries for a combine.

The brewery combine was an emerging trend. It offered small brewers economies of scale and more control of the local market. In just the three years preceding, local brewers in Pittsburgh, Boston and Baltimore had formed combines. In an era when big industrialists were fighting government "trust busters," combines might be seen as just another way to form monopolies, but in the face of encroaching competition by the big national brands, it was almost as if local brewers were circling their wagons—beer wagons, in this case—against an outside threat.[29]

Hammering out the Dayton combine took a few more months, but in February 1904, Adam Schantz emerged as president of the Dayton Breweries Company. Capitalized at $2.5 million, the new company was a grand consolidation that initially included Adam Schantz Brewing, Schantz and Schwind, Schwind Brewery, Stickle's and Wehner Brewing. The initial press report didn't mention Dayton Brewing—the former Sachs-Pruden brewery—but later ones included it. Only N. Thomas Brewing was a holdout, not coming aboard until September 1906 for $800,000. The final arrangement left out only Hollencamp Ale, which survived as a small family brewery in the new giant's shadow.

For its headquarters, Dayton Breweries leased a suite of offices in the new Arcade, making it an original tenant in what would become one of Dayton's most beloved landmarks. Opening in March that year to great fanfare, the Arcade covered a block in the middle of downtown. It was an ensemble of offices, apartments and shops with a central market under a great glass dome. (The Arcade's fortunes rose and fell throughout the twentieth century, but it remains standing as of this writing—long vacant and sadly deteriorated but seeing a renewed effort to restore it.)

While a minority on the board of directors, local brewers held Dayton Breweries' top positions. Under Adam Schantz was his uncle, George, as vice-president; Louis L. Wehner as secretary-treasurer; and Frank Wurfel as superintendent of sales and collections (he had held a similar position at the Schwind brewery). The board also had strong representation from Dayton's brewing clan: besides the officers just named, Michael J. Schwind, president of Schwind Brewery and a son of Coelestin and Christina Schwind, was also a director. Other clan members rotated through.

Schantz claimed the combine had no desire or need to shut down any of the merged breweries. "The increase of the business in the past several years will justify the operation of all the plants," he told the press. Schantz may have meant it, but the first brewery would close in less than two years.

Arcade Building, Third Street Entrance. Dayton, Ohio.

Third Street entrance to the new Dayton Arcade, 1907. *Dayton Postcard Collection, Dayton Metro Library.*

What the company did intend to close were troublesome saloons. In fact, Schantz said, the main reason for the consolidation was to "elevate and regulate the saloon business," including closing them where they weren't wanted. "Time and experience have proved that in the long run saloons in divisions of the city where they are not wanted are not profitable," he said.

Troublesome saloons also antagonized voters, and the temperance movement was pressing states for stronger local option laws. One month after the combine was formed, Ohio passed the Brannock bill, which would allow voters to ban retail beer and liquor sales in local districts. The Anti-Saloon League supported the bill "as far as it goes" but vowed it would "at once renew the fight" for even stronger measures.[30]

BREAKAWAY BREWERS: THE OLT BROTHERS

Combining breweries may have been a defensive move, but it also had the effect, planned or not, of consolidating the beer-related assets of Dayton's brewing clan—the Olts, Schantzes, Schwinds and Wehners. While the combine also included the Stickle, N. Thomas and former Sachs-Pruden breweries, the first four families dominated it.

That said, the clan apparently was less homogenous than it seemed. No sooner did N. Thomas join the Dayton Breweries than the Olt brothers broke out: on November 6, 1906, they formed the Olt Brewing Company. Charles J. Olt, by then forty years old, left his job with Dayton Breweries— he managed the Schantz & Schwind plant—to be the new company's president. William J. Olt (1877–1953)—who had held various jobs in his father's line of work as a butcher, salesman and cashier—became vice-president. Fred Olt (1874–1958), a cashier with Dayton Breweries, became secretary and treasurer.

What prompted the Olt brothers to strike out on their own isn't clear. Big changes were happening at Dayton Breweries in 1906. Despite Adam Schantz's promise, the company ended brewing in Jacob Stickle's outdated brewery and announced plans to end brewing in the Riverside plant. Stickle's would be converted to a bottling works, and Riverside would become an ice plant. Meanwhile, the just-acquired Hydraulic Brewery was getting a major makeover that would more than double its capacity to 150,000 barrels. It isn't clear what drove their decision, but the Olts were the only members of

The former Sachs-Pruden brewery faces South Patterson Boulevard where the Miami and Erie Canal once flowed. *Author's collection.*

the clan who had never had their own brewery, and they held no seats on Dayton Breweries' board of directors.

Whatever drove their need to break away, they seemed to do it without fracturing the combine. If there was any disgruntlement, the local press missed it, and no evidence surfaced that the combine tried to fight their secession. One could wonder if their plan was the subject of pillow talk between Adam Schantz and his wife, their sister Eva, and whether the bond between Adam and Eva was what granted the Olt brothers the forbearance they needed from the combine's chief executive.

Early the next year, they picked a location well to the east of the Dayton Breweries' plants, on the south side of East Second Street between North McGee and North Irwin. Its business address was 34 North McGee. With only $50,000 in capital stock, the Olt brothers' new brewery was a modest plant in a repurposed warehouse. But Olt's Superba Cream Ale and other beers and porters proved popular. In coming years, the Superba brand would put the company literally on the map: as of this writing, Superba Court still runs between McGee and Irwin, a block north of Third.

Dayton seemed to have plenty of thirsty palates, but times were about to change. Like an asteroid still far out in space but in an orbit intersecting Earth's, Prohibition was approaching. Two world wars would rage and men would walk on the moon before Dayton saw another new brewery.[31]

CHAPTER 3

MIAMISBURG

THE STAR CITY

A popular way to travel between Dayton and Cincinnati in the 1880s was on the steel rails of the "Big Four"—the Cleveland, Columbus, Cincinnati and Indianapolis Railway (later the Cleveland, Cincinnati, Chicago and St. Louis Railroad). Chugging north into Miamisburg in southern Montgomery County, passengers would have skirted the east side of the Miami and Erie Canal—just a few decades old, but already a relic from the time when the world traveled at the speed of a towpath mule. To their right, at the foot of a tall hill, would have appeared the bustling Miami Valley Brewery. Passing it, they would have seen—and, if the wind was right, smelled—its horse stables and hog pens and then the brewhouse itself—a two-story structure accompanied by an icehouse, a bottling plant and a wagon shed. A plume of black smoke might have been rising from the chimney of its coal-fired steam plant, rivaling the locomotive's sooty smoke trail.

But in the predawn darkness of Monday, March 25, 1889, passengers would have found themselves being carried toward a frightening scene: the darkness ahead erupting in leaping flames and flying embers glinting on the tracks and lighting up the side of the hill. That morning, fire engulfed the icehouse and attacked the brewery where the proprietor and his family lay sleeping.[32]

More than a century later, hardly anyone remembers what was once a prominent business. Miamisburg, the self-proclaimed "Star City," grew from a village of fewer than three thousand residents in 1890 to a city

Star City Brewing occupies an 1828 building that originally housed a sawmill. *Author's collection.*

of nearly twenty thousand as of this writing, according to U.S. Census records. Situated nine miles south of Dayton and forty miles north of Cincinnati, it became best known for the Miamisburg Mound, a large Adena mound overlooking the valley from atop the hill. Across the road from it rose the Mound nuclear weapons plant, later cleaned up and turned into a business park.

A quarter mile north of the old brewery, as of this writing downtown Miamisburg is reversing decades of slow decline by remaking itself into an entertainment destination. It sports a new Riverfront Park along the levee, a restored movie house on Main Street, new restaurants and two brewpubs just a block apart on South Second Street.

The Star City Brewing Company opened in 2013 in an 1828 building that was originally a sawmill. Longtime residents remember when it was the Peerless Mill Inn, a popular Miamisburg supper club, and the Peerless Pantry even earlier. It had been closed for years after a fire.

The Lucky Star Brewery opened the next year, repurposing a 170-year-old brick building that once housed a farm implement factory. Behind the breweries, parking lots cover what was once the canal.

Star City Brewing took its name deliberately, but Lucky Star's was coincidental. The owner, Glenn Perrine, hailed from Lewisburg, about

Justin Kohnen, proprietor of Star City Brewing. *Author's collection.*

twenty-five miles northwest of Miamisburg, and he registered the name before deciding where to locate his business.

Star City owner Justin Kohnen, a Miamisburg native, said the rich textures of his taproom's stone floor, wooden beams and fireplace give it a rustic charm and prompt questions about its past. "They come in for a beer and they get a history lesson," he said in 2018.

Miamisburg is about as old as Dayton. Virginia pioneer Zachariah Hole and his family settled there in 1797, causing it to be known as "Hole's Station" until other pioneers formally named it in 1818. The river valley served as a corridor connecting it with Dayton and Cincinnati. John W. Harries would have floated through it on a canalboat with his family in 1829 on his way to a career at the Dayton Brewery. In January 1848, Nicholas Thomas would have plodded through town in his stocking feet, carrying his precious boots on his back, on a journey that would lead to the Hydraulic Brewery.

If Thomas had wanted to rest his feet and slake his thirst at a local brewery, he would have found one right along the towpath. The history of brewing in Miamisburg is murky, but it hints at breweries early in its history. Warren Jenkins's 1839 *Ohio Gazetteer, and Traveler's Guide* listed "one brewery" among its manufacturing concerns.[33]

The Brewery at City Hall

The earliest official reference to a Miamisburg brewery is a series of 1848 Montgomery County deed transfer records describing a property as "the brewery lot." It lay on the west side of the canal in the first block north of Market Street. Modern maps would have placed it on the east side of North First Street in the first block north of Central Avenue, under the block-long campus of Miamisburg's municipal offices. The records imply it was well known, hinting a brewery might have been standing there for years— possibly the one mentioned back in 1839. If so, it would make Miamisburg's city hall the site of its first brewery.

The records show the property changed hands several times in 1848 until someone identified as Charles "Schrader" bought it from Erhard Deutch for $1,800. No "Schrader" appears on the handwritten population census sheets of 1850 or 1860, but the 1850 census of industrial products in Miami Township bears the scrawled name of a brewer similar to Schrader's. Likewise, the township's 1850 population census recorded a "Charles Schrider" as a brewer. It further identified him as a German immigrant, born circa 1824, with a wife named Catharine and a daughter, Eloise, born just that year. "Charles Schrauder" was

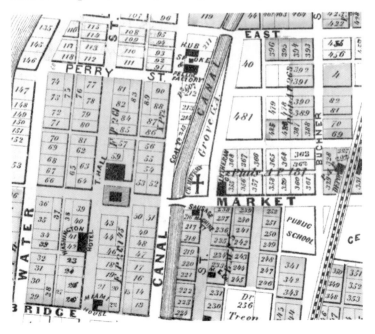

Miamisburg's first brewery of record stood on what was later a coal yard north of Market (now East Central). *From Combination Atlas Map of Montgomery County, Ohio (1875).*

the sole brewer listed for Miamisburg in *W.W. Reilly & Co.'s Ohio State Business Directory for 1853–4*. Those are the earliest records found naming a Miamisburg brewer.

Whatever the correct spelling, Schrader sold the property to William and Jacob Wenz that year for $4,500—more than twice what he'd paid for it, suggesting he'd built up a good business, improved the property or both. Even less turned up about William and Jacob, who in turn sold the brewery a few years later, apparently to start anew in Dayton. The 1860 census for Dayton found two brewers there with the same first names and the last name "Wentz," along with several family members. Records show nothing more about the brewery they left behind.

WILLIAM NUSZ AND HIS BREWERIES

Another brewery was up and running at least by 1860. *George W. Hawes' Ohio State Gazetteer and Business Directory for 1860–61* listed "Nutz & Herrmann" as proprietors of the Miamisburg Brewery on River Street. News articles, ancestry databases and county land records suggest "Nutz" was G. William Nusz (1825–1881), an immigrant from Heuchelheim, Bavaria, later in central Germany. Nusz's obituary in the *Miamisburg Bulletin* reported he emigrated in 1849 and arrived in Miamisburg in 1852.

Land records indicate "Herrmann" refers to John (1810–1877) or his son, Phillip (born circa 1835). The name frequently appeared as "Harman" or "Herman" in ancestry and land records. How Nusz found the Herrmanns is unclear, but the reason might have been John's daughter, Margaret (1839–1902); she and Nusz were married in 1854. The brewery seems to have followed as a family business.

Little could be found about John Herrmann, but land records show that in 1849 he bought a lot between the east bank of the river and the west side of Water Street, later Miami, just south of Ferry. In 1856, two years after gaining Nusz as a son-in-law, he bought lots just south of his, extending his land halfway down the block. This is where Herrmann apparently built a brewery. Land records show it was there by the middle of 1860, when he sold most of the land for a dollar to his son and daughter, Phillip Herrmann and Margaret Nusz, including "all personal property belonging to the brewery which stands on the above described real estate." A part of Miamisburg's Riverfront Park now covers the site.

No records surfaced naming John Herrmann as a brewer. The 1850 census lists him as a laborer. The "Nutz and Herrmann" of 1860 more likely referred to Nusz and Phillip Herrmann, then twenty-four—old enough to be William's junior partner. By the end of 1867, ads appeared in the *Miamisburg Bulletin* for "Miamisburg Brewery and Malt House." But they only listed Nusz as proprietor. He offered countywide distribution under certain conditions: "Beer will be promptly delivered to order, at any point in the county—if wanted in sufficient quantity to warrant."

The next year, John Herrmann transferred his original lot to William and Margaret Nusz, and Phillip Herrmann transferred his share of the brewery to them. The 1870 census found John "Harman," by then sixty-one, working as a farmer. Census takers in 1870 and 1880 found Phillip Harman working as a butcher and living on Main Street with a growing family, but his name also faded from the records.

Census takers in 1870 found a George Harman, fifty-three, of Germany, boarding with the Nusz family and working in the brewery. Ditto for Jacob Alexander, twenty-two, a native of Bavaria. Whether George Harman was really a Herrmann, and what became of him, is uncertain. Jacob Alexander (1848–1914) had just immigrated in 1869. He married William and Margaret's daughter, Wilhelmina (1857–1922), in 1875, and Jacob worked at the brewery for several years before he also turned to farming.[34]

Undated photo of August V. Kuehn (*left*) with his daughter, Marie, and others unknown, somewhere in Europe. *Jann Kuehn Adams Collection.*

The brewery and malt house must have done well. In 1873, Nusz was able to buy several acres just south of town between the canal and the hill. He platted a subdivision with three lots that became the site of the new Miami Valley Brewery. As with the earlier breweries, all signs of it are gone. Plat maps show it stood on land south of Mound Avenue and east of South Main Street. Miamisburg's Community Park occupies the site as of this writing.

While John and Phillip didn't stay with the business, Nusz owned and operated the brewery until he died at age fifty-five on July 27, 1881. He made beer in Miamisburg longer than any other known brewer, and his funeral drew grieving friends from surrounding towns. The Apollo Band of Hamilton, which performed at major events in that city, made the twenty-mile trip to Miamisburg to play at his funeral. William Nusz's burial was at Hillgrove Cemetery, where the Herrmann and Nusz families share a tall monument on high ground.

Jacob Alexander, Nusz's son-in-law, remained with the brewery at least until 1880, but Margaret Nusz sold it in 1882. State records show the Miami Valley Brewing Company was incorporated that year, capitalized at $50,000, but it changed hands twice before a slightly more familiar brewer bought it in 1883 for $21,000.[35]

AUGUST KUEHN AND MIAMI VALLEY BREWING

August Victor Kuehn (1848–1913) was born in Ammerschwihr, a small town in Alsace, northeastern France near the Rhine River. His passport application described him as about five feet, nine inches tall, with hazel eyes and a Grecian nose. He immigrated in 1872 and followed the well-worn brewer's path to Cincinnati. He first appeared in the 1875 *Williams' Cincinnati Directory*, and subsequent directories found him working for the Jackson Brewery until 1883. He married Catherine Theureling there in 1877.

Kuehn left Cincinnati for Miamisburg just as the Jackson Brewery was falling on hard times: by 1884, it was in the hands of the Hamilton County Court of Insolvency.

Kuehn bought the old Nusz brewery and the three lots it occupied. An 1886 Sanborn insurance map shows a two-thousand-barrel-per-year plant with ten buildings including an attached malt house and icehouse, with a bottling plant nearby. Storage cellars were under the brewery and in the foot of the hill.

Undated photo of August V. Kuehn (*second from right in front row*) at his Marietta Brewery. *Washington County (Ohio) Historical Society.*

Kuehn and his family were at home on the morning of the fire in 1889. Flames first appeared in the icehouse adjoining the coal furnace, according to the March 29, 1889 *Miamisburg Bulletin.* The fire consumed the bottling works, malt house and "the whole upper floor of the establishment with a suite of six rooms occupied by Mr. Kuehn's family," the paper reported. It went on: "Had the fire broken out at midnight the whole family might have perished, and Mrs. Kuehn has determined to live hereafter in town."

The paper painted a dire picture of the aftermath. "What was one of the most complete and substantial structures of its kind in the Miami Valley is now a blackened heap of ruins," it reported. But it struck a hopeful tone: "As soon as the loss is adjusted by the insurance companies, the work of rebuilding will be commenced and hurried to completion. Meanwhile Mr. Kuehn…has made every arrangement to supply the rapidly increasing demand for the wholesome beverage, made at the Miami Valley Brewery, with usual regularity."

But Kuehn went back to Cincinnati, the *Bulletin*'s April 12 edition reported. The Jackson Brewery apparently was recovering: the 1890 *Williams' Cincinnati Directory* found Kuehn working there as its foreman. Census records and city directories show he eventually settled in Marietta, Ohio, where he joined with two other men to buy an old beer plant and reopen it as the Marietta Brewery. He became its president before dying in 1913. He was forgotten there in time, but in recent years a new Marietta brewpub revived his legacy by taking the name of his old brewery. As of this writing, one wall of the new Marietta Brewing Company is the canvas for a life-size mural, based on a photo, depicting Kuehn and several family members seated on barrels in front of his brewery. His great-granddaughter, Jann Kuehn Adams, author of *German Marietta and Washington County* (Arcadia Publishing, 2016,) leads local history tours that include the brewery and stories about her ancestor.

In Miamisburg, Kuehn faded into obscurity like Schrader and Nusz before him, but a sketch of the brewery in his name survives on an 1886 lithograph of the town. It was reprinted in 1980. As of this writing, lithographs with tiny images of "A. Kuehn's Brewery" adorn walls of homes and businesses around town, including Star City Brewing.

MIAMISBURG BREWING COMPANY

The brewery's history for the next few years is unknown, but records indicate it was up and running again by 1892. A Sanborn map of that year shows the plant reorganized but with essentially the same footprint, operating as the Miamisburg Brewing Company. The main difference was the bottling plant: the old one was gone and a new plant stood north of the brewhouse, separate but still connected by a steam line from the brewery's boiler. It was labeled "Miamisburg Star Bottling Co." Miamisburg Brewing was incorporated on October 6 of that year, and the bottling plant was incorporated two years later as a separate entity bottling wine, beer and ale.[36]

The reincorporation coincided with a new owner. Kuehn sold the brewery to Henry P. Duescher of Hamilton. Deuscher was a native of Baden, Germany, who became the principal of H.P. Deuscher & Company, a malting company in Hamilton. Whether he had a prior connection with the Miamisburg brewery is unknown, but the May 10, 1900 *Miamisburg News* named him as its principal owner.

Duescher remained in Hamilton, city directories and census records show, but in 1895 Henry B. Graf, secretary of Deuscher's Hamilton company, moved to Miamisburg to manage the brewery. He occupied a house up the hill, where he apparently raised goats on the side. "Messrs. Dan Young of Hotel Young and Henry Graf, manager of the Miamisburg Brewery, have gone into the goat business," the August 29, 1899 *Dayton Daily News* reported. "The farm is on the brewery hill. It behooves the citizens of Miamisburg to keep all newspapers, shoes and wearing apparel well locked up, and to have signs on their gate posts, 'Beware of the Goats.'"[37]

THE FINAL FIRE

Under Deuscher's ownership and Graf's management, Miamisburg Brewing appeared to prosper. It ordered a twenty-ton ice machine in 1898. The August 3, 1899 *Miamisburg News* carried a page-one ad announcing "absolutely pure" ice was about to be for sale. The brewery would soon be on the front page again—not for ice this time, but for fire.

Julius Smith, a carpenter employed by the brewery, was at work shortly before noon on Tuesday, May 8, 1900, when he spotted flames in the stable on the south side of the brewery, according to the May 10 *Miamisburg News*. Smith called all hands to fight the fire, but a strong wind fanned the blaze. Five horses trapped in the stable were burned alive.

"In ten minutes the stable was a solid mass of fire, and the terrific wind quickly communicated the fire to the frame addition of the brewery building," the paper reported. The addition housed the new ice plant.

A smokestack behind a passing locomotive marks the site of the old Miamisburg Brewing Company. *Miamisburg Historic Lantern Slides, Dayton Metro Library.*

The brewery's staff fought the fire with a hose and buckets. The wind-whipped flames made it a perilous task. One worker, Bernard Wieland, was throwing water on the burning stable when "the wind blew a sheet of flame right into his face," the *News* reported, adding it left him "severely burned about the head and hands." (Wieland apparently survived, as he shows up again in the 1910 census.) Another hand reported fighting the flames was the brewery's fireman, William Harman—Phillip Herrmann's son, according to census records.

The brewery lay outside the village line, but Miamisburg's fire department turned out to help. Firefighters and brewery workers saved the brewery foreman's home just east of the brewery and the frame building of the bottling plant. But the brewery was lost, and the fate of "three or four thousand barrels of beer" in several cellars was unknown, the *News* reported.

Suspicion of the fire's cause immediately turned to embers from a Big Four locomotive that had barreled past the brewery minutes earlier. "This is mere supposition, but it is generally accepted in the 'Burg,'" the *Dayton Daily News* observed.

Fires weren't new to the brewery. The *Miamisburg News* report mentioned two previous blazes. But this was the final blow. With breweries proliferating up the canal in Dayton, Miamisburgers wouldn't lack for beer. But they wouldn't enjoy their own hometown brew for more than a century.[38]

CHAPTER 4

XENIA AND TROY

TIES TO DAYTON

The shared German heritage of Dayton's brewing families helped bind them together in a virtual clan. But this interconnectedness seems largely confined to the city. Research found few connections between brewers or breweries in different towns. Two notable exceptions were the breweries in Xenia, fifteen miles east in Greene County, and Troy, twenty miles north in Miami.

XENIA AND THE HOLLENCAMPS

Xenia's brewing history goes back at least as far as Dayton's, and historical accounts suggest Xenia was the first settlement in the Dayton region to have a brewery. It seems only fitting, since Xenia's settlers named their town with a Greek word for hospitality. William Gordon moved to Xenia from Warren County in 1805 and built "a small log house, the first brewery in Xenia," according to M.A. Broadstone's *History of Greene County, Ohio*. Gordon's brewery stood on the northeast corner of Water and Whiteman Streets, later Third and Whiteman. Broadstone didn't say how long the brewery existed, and no records were found that revealed its fate.

The name that stands out in Xenia's brewing history is Bernard Hollencamp (circa 1813–1872), the German immigrant who first teamed up with Henry Ferneding in Dayton in 1852. Greene County land records

HOLLENCAMP BROS. BREWERS & MALTSTERS
COR. SECOND & COLUMBUS STS. XENIA, OHIO

Illustration of the Hollencamp brewery. *From* Greene County Atlas *(1874)*.

show they bought the Xenia Brewery from James Kyle (1824–1887), disputing some accounts that say Ferneding and Hollencamp founded the brewery.

In August 1853, Kyle bought two lots for $600 at the northwest corner of Water and Ankeny Streets, later Third and Columbus, three blocks east of Whiteman. The deed transfer record describes the premises as "commonly known as the Xenia Brewery," implying a brewery already stood there. But Kyle apparently made substantial improvements before advertising it for sale less than six months later. His ad in the January 11, 1854 *Xenia Torchlight* describes the brewery as "built of brick—and nearly new—with an extensive capacity for malting and brewing." It called it "the only establishment of its kind in the county" and said it came with "an extensive and profitable business."

Kyle didn't say why he wanted to sell it, but the deed transfer record shows Hollencamp and Ferneding paid $8,000 for it in September 1854—a more than thirteen-fold increase from what Kyle had paid just over a year earlier, not counting whatever he invested in improvements.

Hollencamp and Ferneding owned the brewery together for three years. Hollencamp bought Ferneding's half-interest for $10,000 in September 1857—another soaring increase. How much business they were doing is unknown. By 1870, the brewery was turning out 1,472 barrels of beer and 400 barrels of ale, according to a census of industrial output taken that year.

The brewery apparently was doing well. In 1871, Hollencamp had a fine house built at 339 East Second Street, on the southwest corner of Second and Columbus. The two-story brick dwelling stood immediately north of the brewery's single-story office. Beyond the office stood the two attached buildings of the brewery itself, which stretched downhill along Columbus to Third. The modest plant was the only one in town, apparently

RES. OF HOLLENCAMP BROS.
COR. SECOND & COLUMBUS STS. XENIA. GREENE CO. OHIO

Illustration of the Hollencamp house. *From* Greene County Atlas *(1874).*

sufficient to meet local demand. The brewery and office are gone, but as of this writing Hollencamp's richly detailed, Victorian Italianate house still stands—listed in the National Register of Historic Places but vacant and sorely in need of repair.

Two of Hollencamp's sons, Bernard Jr. (circa 1848–1881) and Frank (born circa 1852), joined their father in the brewing business. Nephew Theodore Hollenkamp also started working there. When Bernard Sr. died in 1872, his sons kept it going as Hollencamp Brothers, with Theodore as an employee. They sold beer, ales and malt, according to an ad in the January 21, 1874 *Xenia Daily Gazette*. Theodore left for Dayton sometime between 1882 and 1885.[39]

THE WOMAN'S CRUSADE AND THE SHADES OF DEATH

Annie Wittenmyer (1827–1900) was born Sarah "Annie" Turner in Sandy Springs, Adams County. Well educated and progressive, she was a part of the social reform movement that exploded across America in the women's temperance crusade of 1874. When the Woman's Christian Temperance Union formed that year in Cleveland, she became its first president. In *History of the Woman's Temperance Crusade*, Wittenmyer described Xenia as "the pride of southern Ohio" but said the town of ten thousand people had 120 drinking places—"one saloon to eighty-three inhabitants." (*Williams' Xenia City Directory for 1870–71* listed twenty-three saloons.)

In mid-February 1884, as the temperance crusade spread from town to town across Ohio, crusaders in Xenia took over Whiteman Street. Nine saloons lined it—five in a space of three hundred yards. The *New York Herald* reported these five places had gained "an unenviable reputation, and are known about town as 'Shades of Death,' 'Mule's Ear,' 'Hell's Half Acre,' 'Certain Death,' and 'Devil's Den.' For three days the ladies have labored almost incessantly in front of the 'Shades of Death,' which is considered the backbone" of them all.

Shades of Death was a brick house on a corner at Whiteman and Second Streets. News reports identified its proprietor as Stephen Phillips, although no saloon keeper by that name appears in Xenia directories. At Shades of Death, men—women weren't allowed—would gather in a deep cellar to drink and gamble, according to *New York Herald* and *Cincinnati Gazette* reports Wittenmyer excerpted in her book. On February 13, the crusaders descended on the dive and posted themselves outside its doors. They prayed and sang day after day, sometimes in falling snow. Phillips held out grimly until 2:00 p.m. on February 19, when, as the *Herald* reported, "he opened his doors, invited the ladies in and announced his unconditional surrender. After prayers, he rolled the barrels of liquor into the street and smashed them in, amid hymns, prayers, and great excitement."

The hometown *Gazette* reported Phillips dumped out "a half-barrel of blackberry brandy, the same of highwines, a few kegs of beer, and some bottles of ale and whiskey." Phillips, it reported, turned his saloon into a meat market.

The Xenia crusade went on for several weeks. Wittenmyer wrote twenty-five saloons eventually closed, some forever. The Hollencamp Brothers brewery didn't escape the women's attention. Wittenmyer cited one incident there as an example of how "the liquor element became defiant and insulting." As a group stood outside the brewery one day, she wrote, "a man

The Hollencamp house in 2018. *Author's collection.*

came out with a mug of beer in his hands, and stopping a woman in the midst of her prayer, offered her a drink; holding out the foaming beer, he told her it was Jesus."[40]

Hollencamp Brothers survived the crusade, but Beers's *History of Montgomery County* hints of trouble in the late 1870s. In July 1878, Ferneding—by then sixty-five years of age, with decades of experience in a wide range of businesses—was appointed an assignee of the brewery and charged with "putting their affairs on a good footing." Beers didn't describe the nature of the brewery's trouble, but it might have marked a difficult time of transition. Bernard Hollencamp Jr. died in 1881, and Frank died sometime earlier—exactly when isn't known, but his brother's will of 1881 describes him as already deceased.

During the 1880s, the brewery became known as the "Hollencamp Company" and the "Hollencamp Brewing Co." It was bottling its brews by 1885, if not much sooner, and its ales seemed to be in demand as far as Cincinnati. Noted the July 7, 1885 *Xenia Daily Gazette*, "The Hollencamp Co. made another large shipment of 40 dozen bottles of their ale to Cincinnati, this morning. They have shipped over 300 dozen bottles to Cincinnati within the past two months."

The company ordered a refrigerated storage building at the end of 1889. The December 9 *Gazette* reported it cost $8,000 to $10,000. The 1896 and 1898 editions of the *Brewer's Guide* reported the brewery was producing three to four thousand barrels of ale, porter and lager beer per year.

The transition from Hollencamp Brothers to later owners is murky, but Henry Ferneding wasn't the only Dayton brewer to take an interest in the business. In 1892, George Abraham Weddle dissolved his partnership with Nick Thomas in the Hydraulic Brewery to join the Hollencamp company, making it Hollencamp and Weddle. Just five years later, it became the Hollencamp Bottling Company, according to the April 22, 1897 *Xenia Gazette*. "They have ceased making beer and hereafter will devote their attention to the manufacture of ale, etc., and will act as agent for the Milwaukee beer," the paper added. Other records indicate the correct name was Hollencamp Brewing and Bottling—it was still brewing ale, after all. The "Milwaukee beer" went unnamed, but Hollencamp apparently was ceding its lager beer market to Schlitz, one of the national brands showing up in Dayton.[41]

Turning the Century

Xenia's only brewery staggered through the turn of the century. In August 1899, land records show, both state and federal tax collectors seized Hollencamp Brewing and Bottling's assets and sold them at auction. Ironically, the seizure and sale put the brewery back into Hollencamp hands—those of Henry Hollencamp (1850–1929), a wealthy Dayton clothier who was distantly related to the Hollencamp brewers.

Henry Hollencamp had diverse business interests, including ice and cold storage, an industry closely related to brewing. In March 1899, he had formed the Xenia Brewing and Artificial Ice Company as an Indiana corporation with other investors, including Daniel J. Hollencamp (1863–1941), the youngest of Bernard Hollencamp Sr.'s sons. It isn't clear whether the brewery was still making ale by this time. Daniel J.'s interest was in the rapidly emerging refrigeration industry, and this launched his career as a refrigeration engineer. The company decided to build a big ice-making plant on the brewery site. But whatever Henry and Daniel planned for the brewery suddenly faced a new challenge.

On September 3, 1901, Xenia held a local option election to prohibit the sale of alcohol, and citizens voted overwhelmingly to go dry. The count was 1,116 for and 651 against; all but one of the city's seven wards favored it. The result "was a great surprise, even to the temperance people," who had expected to win by a narrow margin, the *Dayton Daily News* reported the next day. Following state law, the issue would have to go to the city council for final action, but the outcome wasn't in serious doubt. "It is safe to say that the councilman who votes 'wet' has seen his last term in that body," the paper observed.[42]

Plans for the new ice plant progressed. The *Xenia Gazette* of January 9, 1902, reported it would replace the brewery's ten-tons-per-day ice plant with one making up to sixty tons daily. As for the brewery itself, the August 20, 1903 *Xenia Gazette and Torchlight* reported it would manufacture "temperance beer" under the name Brinkle and Reading, with L.L. Reading as president; Henry Hollencamp, vice-president; C.W. Brinkle, secretary-treasurer; and Edward H. Fallows, director.

The *American Brewers' Review* described Fallows, of New York, as a son of Bishop Samuel Fallows of Chicago, developer of the non-alcoholic "Bishop's beer." In February 1895, Bishop Fallows had opened what he considered the antidote to the traditional Chicago saloon: a "home salon," replete with "all the regulation features of the grog-shop with the single important exception

Beer wagons in front of the Henne brewery between 1875 and 1890. *Troy Historical Society.*

of the intoxicating liquor," according to the September 1895 *Homiletic Review*, a pastoral magazine. The featured beverage was Fallows' Bishop's Beer.

But Brinkle and Reading was quickly on the ropes: the November 1904 *American Brewers' Review* reported it in receivership. "The company started in the manufacture of temperance beer, and then turned to making the ordinary grades of beer," it reported. State law allowed brewers in a dry district to produce alcohol for sale outside the district, but the specific circumstances for Brinkle and Reading aren't clear.[43]

Once again, the brewery was in dire straits. Tax collectors had seized it once before. This time, Brinkle and Reading hit on a novel way to avoid a repeat. On June 30, 1905, as reported in the *New York Sun*, "The sewers of Xenia were flushed today with hundreds of barrels of beer. This was because of the visit of a government inspector from Dayton to the Brinkle and Reading Brewery, which for several months had been in the hands of a receiver. The owners preferred to forfeit the beer rather than pay a government tax."[44]

It was a bitter farewell toast to beer brewing in Xenia. But Devil Wind Brewing opened more than a century later, giving a nod to the city's brewing heritage by naming its Helles lager "Hollencamp."

Troy and Titus Schwind

Established in Miami County in 1808 and designated as Miami County's seat of government the same year, Troy saw rapid growth, soon boosted by the Miami and Erie Canal, which cut through the middle of town. Its claims to fame would include Hobart, a food equipment manufacturer founded in 1897; the WACO Aircraft Company, the world's biggest airplane maker in the 1930s; and the Hayner Distilling Company, founded in 1866 by Lewis Hayner.

Troy's brewing history is less well remembered. One local history book asserts brewing came to Troy as early as 1841, but the first brewer of record arrived later. He was Titus Schwind (1820–1879), the Bavarian immigrant whose three brothers all settled in Dayton. Unlike his brothers—who employed spouses, siblings and children in their Dayton breweries—Titus apparently never married, and he was sole proprietor of the brewery at 111 West Water Street, where part of the building still stands as of this writing.

Exactly when Schwind started brewing, and where, isn't clear. Dayton news articles and history books indicate Titus's younger brothers, Coelestin and Anton, brewed with him somewhere in Troy in the late 1840s before joining Joseph, the eldest of the four, back in Dayton in 1850. The 1850

Undated photo of Henne brewery employees. *Troy Historical Society.*

census for Troy, taken in August, shows Titus already established as a brewer, but it gives no residence or place of business. County land records show he paid $400 for the West Water Street lot in 1854 but not whether any structures stood on it. An Ohio historic inventory of the original plat of Troy, completed in 2006, dates the brewery to 1863—with the important caveat that it couldn't guarantee the accuracy of any details.

Whether on Water Street or elsewhere, records indicate Schwind had a brewery in Troy for at least a quarter century before selling it in 1874. During those years, he expanded his operation considerably five blocks west, on a wedge of land bounded by Water Street on the north, Main on the south, Cherry on the east and straddling what was then Jackson Street. The southwest corner of the property edged the Miami and Erie Canal at Lock 12 South. In 2018, the Ohio Historical Society dedicated a historical marker on the restored site of Lock 12. In 2019, Kettering Health Network opened a new hospital on the old brewery site.

Schwind sold it all for $12,000 in 1874, the same year of the temperance crusade. One local author assumed the February crusade influenced his

Undated view of the Henne Brewery from above. *Troy Historical Society.*

decision. "[N]o doubt Schwind was glad to sell out," Thomas Bemis Wheeler wrote in *Troy: The Nineteenth Century*. But Troy's crusade appeared mild compared to those in Xenia and elsewhere. Wittenmyer barely mentioned it in her book, although she noted local women formed a Temperance League, and 737 people signed a pledge to "make common cause against the common enemy, intemperance."[45]

Another possible reason was failing health. Census and estate records show Schwind moved down to Dayton and lived his last years with the family of his brother Coelestin. The will he wrote in 1877 directed $1,200 go to Coelestin "for the care he and his family have taken of me during my stay with him and for the trouble and expense I have caused him in my illness." Five years after selling his brewery, Titus died in Coelestin's mansion at age fifty-nine.

More than a century after his death, Titus Schwind has all but vanished from Troy's history. But he was well known at the time: more than one hundred citizens rode a special train to Dayton for his funeral, according to his obituary in the January 27, 1879 *Dayton Journal*. There they joined another crowd of relatives and friends. Coelestin's fourteen-room brick mansion "was unable to hold the half of them," the paper reported. The German Pioneer Society, of which Titus had been a member, led an "unusually long" funeral procession to Dayton's historic Woodland Cemetery, where he joined his brothers Joseph and Anton.[46]

HENNE AND MAYER

The new owners were Joseph Henne and John George Mayer. Born in Württemberg, Henne (1831–1890) immigrated at age eighteen. He owned a Troy boot and shoe business for several years before deciding to become a brewer. Mayer (1837–1896) was a Bavarian transplant who reached Troy by way of Cincinnati in 1861. Mayer worked as a barber, confectioner and grocer before jumping into the brewing business with Henne.

The partnership lasted three years. Mayer sold out to Henne in 1877 to become a dealer in wines, liquors and beer, according to land records and a biographical sketch in *The History of Miami County*. He also bottled beer and charged soda fountains. Mayer's trade might have exacted a high price: he died at age fifty-nine of cirrhosis of the liver, according to a county death record.[47]

The old Titus Schwind (later Henne) brewery was vacant in 2018. *Author's collection.*

Joseph Henne continued the brewing business. In July 1884, Joseph sold half his interest to his son Jacob (1861–1914), and they operated as "Joseph Henne & Son." Historical photos show the brewery as a narrow, three-story brick building with a chimney at the back and an attached, two-story building on its east side. In addition to the brewery and additional facilities five blocks west, at some point they added a large pond and icehouse south of town, between the canal and a millrace. In the winter, the Hennes would harvest ice off the pond for their beer cellars. They also sold it commercially, sometimes loading canalboats with ice for destinations to the south.

With Joseph's death in 1890, Jacob inherited his father's share of the business. It continued to grow, and Jacob knew how to build brand loyalty. Wheeler noted, "Jacob Henne was often in the habit of going from one saloon to another to check up on the sale of his beer and occasionally to buy a round of beers for everyone in the house." In the 1890s, Jacob built a new, much larger brewery at 614 West Water, on the same square with the malt house and the cellars. The new brewery could turn out four to five thousand barrels, according to the 1898 *Brewer's Guide*.

The old brewery saw a series of owners. Sometime after 1900, fire damaged both attached structures. They were cut off above the second floor and capped with a flat roof, resulting in an unimposing, two-story building. New owners renovated it as The Brewery restaurant in the 1970s, and it functioned as a bar before closing in 2017.

Jacob Henne died at age fifty-four as a prominent local business leader. He was a director of the Troy National Bank and a member of several associations. He outlived the brewery, which became a victim of the growing anti-saloon movement. In November 1908, Miami County's temperance proponents took advantage of Ohio's new Rose law to vote the county dry.

Henne closed his brewery the next spring. On April 23, the brewery drained its beer down a sewer pipe into the canal. Men and boys grabbed "old cans, bottles and any kind of a receptacle" to catch some, according to that day's *Dayton Daily News*. It added, "For the four hours it poured out of a sewer pipe used to convey refuse of all kinds from the brewery, more half-drunken men and boys were seen than have been arrested since the city went dry."[48]

CHAPTER 5

GOING DRY, STAYING WET

PIQUA AND SIDNEY

PIQUA

Located at a great bow in the Miami River, Piqua lies twenty miles north of Dayton and sixty miles north of Cincinnati. It's Miami County's most northern city. Despite its remoteness, it was one of the first towns in the Miami Valley to have a brewing industry. Unlike Troy, the county seat five miles south, and Sidney, ten miles north in Shelby County, Piqua didn't have one dominant brewery over its history, but several small ones instead.

Settlers first gathered along the river at the southern end of the bow, where its course bends from west to south, according to John A. Rayner's *The First Century of Piqua*. At the top of the bend, near the corner of what became East Water and Harrison Streets, John Manning built the town's first gristmill in 1804. Charles Manning—his relationship to John is unknown—built a small distillery across the river in 1805. The mill and distillery were at the opposite ends of a ford where travelers crossed the river before Piqua had bridges.

Charles Manning sold his distillery in 1807 to Henry Orbison, a settler from Virginia. Orbison sold it five years later and left to fight in the War of 1812, Rayner wrote.

Orbison also brewed beer at his distillery, according to a historical review in the 1875 *Illustrated Historical Atlas of Miami County, Ohio*. It was

The Ohio to Indiana Trail crosses the Great Miami River on a former railroad bridge. Henry Orbison's brewery was said to have been somewhere near the far end. *Author's collection.*

among the first breweries in the Miami Valley—about as old as George Newcom's in Dayton and William Gordon's in Xenia. It didn't last long: sometime after Orbison sold it, construction of a railroad line obliterated the site. (The former railroad was later converted to the Ohio to Indiana recreational trail.)[49]

Piqua saw a surge of breweries in the mid-1830s, a time when the Miami and Erie Canal was coming up from Dayton and the town's population was growing rapidly—more than doubling from about 690 in 1830 to 1,480 in 1840. The breweries mainly clustered between the river and the canal. John Suttle had a brewery in about 1835 on an island in the river at the northeast corner of town, according to Rayner. Land records also show Charles Lorch and John P. Rothaas (or Rathhaas) had a brewery by 1835 just east of the canal on North Spring Street, between East Greene and East North. Rayner mentioned C. Ross, Thomas Bellas and Tuttle and Porter as other brewers of that period, but no other records of their breweries were found.[50]

BEALL AND WESTON

Another shadowy pair is Beall and Weston. Rayner wrote they "had a distillery and brewery just west of the lock and north of the lock mill in 1837." Research revealed few details about them, but Gideon Beall (died in 1837) and Washington A. Weston (1814–1876) moved to Dayton from Alexandria, Virginia, in 1828 and then to Piqua about 1835, according to John F. Edgar's *Pioneer Life in Dayton and Vicinity*. Beall was married to Weston's sister, Ann. Not much else could be learned about him except he died in Piqua prior to the end of 1839. Weston was just fifteen when he arrived in Dayton. W.H. McIntosh's *History of Darke County, Ohio*, describes him as the orphaned son of a sea captain who had perished in the deep, and a mother who had died soon after. Weston started a business in Piqua about 1835, "but the financial crisis of 1836–1837 swept away every dollar he possessed," McIntosh wrote.

This was also about when Beall died. Weston moved on to Greenville, where he eventually founded Farmers National Bank, but in 1851 he sold a Piqua property to John L. Schneyer. It lay between Water Street and the river across from the south end of Spring Street. It came "with the distillery and brewery," according to the deed transfer record. Located a half block east of the canal lock, it isn't clear whether Beall and Weston's brewery was actually there, not west of the canal as Rayner wrote, or whether Rayner's reference was to some otherwise unrecorded brewery. But the small parcel would hold a brewery under a series of owners for decades to come.[51]

HARTMAN PLOCH

The canal opened between Cincinnati and Piqua in 1837, and it opened to Lake Erie in 1845. Piqua continued to grow. The 1840s also saw a new wave of German immigrants spread up the valley, with many settling in Piqua. By 1860, the population had reached 4,616.

One of those immigrants was Hartman Ploch (1819–1881), born in Bavaria and married to Mary Klipstein, also from Bavaria, according to census records and business directories. Ploch and another German immigrant, John Franz (1816–1855), bought the old Rothaas/Rathhaas and Lorch property in 1851. In January 1859, Ploch bought two acres of land for a lagering cellar in Spring Creek Township on the east side of the river, just north of

Illustration of Schneyer's Spring Street Brewery at Spring and Water in Piqua, about 1875. *From* Illustrated Historical Atlas of Miami County, Ohio.

the Ash Street bridge. They were doing business as the City Brewery at least by 1867, when Redfield and Logan's *Columbus & Indianapolis Central Railway Business Guide* identified it by that name. It gave their products as "beer, ale, lager and malt." Census records show Franz's eldest child, twenty-five-year-old Christian, was working in the brewery by 1870, along with Ploch's eldest son, nineteen-year-old William. *R.C. Hellrigle & Co.'s Piqua Directory* for 1875 identified "C. Franz, W. Ploch" as the proprietors and Hartman Ploch as a brewer, indicating Christian and William were running the business by then.[52]

Hartman Ploch still owned the land, and he apparently built more facilities near his lagering cellar. In September 1879, he leased the property to John Butcher Jr. (1855–1913) and Peter Mittler (1841–1925). The lease included "all the buildings, cellars and ponds" located there.

Born in Newport, Kentucky, Butcher was the son of German immigrant Johann Butscher, who had run a small brewery in Newport in the 1860s before partnering with George Wiedemann Sr. to start what would become Newport's best-known beer. Both the younger Butcher and Mittler lived for a few years in Newport and Cincinnati. *Williams' Newport Directory for 1872–1873* listed them as workers for Butcher and Wiedemann.

A few years later, they set off to establish their own brewery. They found Ploch's property in Piqua available, and it was the leading brewery in town at the time. Frederick William Salem's *Beer, Its History and Its Economic Value as a National Beverage* reported it sold 1,200 barrels in 1878 and 1,254 barrels in 1879 (the year Butcher and Mittler leased it). This was about a third more than the sales of the next biggest Piqua brewery.

But the partnership didn't last. Mittler soon left for parts uncertain. A Peter Mittler of the same age, with an identical family, also became Minster's first official brewmaster (see chapter 6), but their histories conflict. His replacement was Christopher Fryer (or Freyer), who in turn left in 1880.[53]

Butcher took on a new partner in 1880, Henry (or Heinrich) Schneider, an immigrant from Reinberg, a village in what was then Prussia, later in the state of Mecklenburg–West Pomerania in northeastern Germany. Schneider (1841–1903) had come to America with his parents at age fifteen, according to his obituary. If anyone deserved a beer, Schneider did: he had served with the Fifth Ohio Cavalry during the Civil War, was captured by Confederate troops and held in the infamous Andersonville Prison. After the war, he lived in Cincinnati until moving to Piqua and replacing Fryer at the brewery. Schneider bought out Butcher's interest a few years later, and Butcher returned to Kentucky, where city directories show he ran a saloon in Bellevue.

Schneider apparently consolidated the brewery operations on the east bank of the river. A brief business article in 1890 reported the brewery could turn out five thousand barrels per year. By 1892, Schneider's plant included a three-story frame building on the east bank of the river near the lagering cellar.

Schneider's new brewery site was ideal—in fact, it was downright scenic, according to a business profile in the March 3, 1896 *Piqua Journal and Daily Dispatch*:

Henry Schneider's brewery on the east bank of the Great Miami River, around 1890. *Piqua Public Library.*

> *His brewery is situated near the Ash street bridge in a romantic location having a handsome reservoir of water, which is several feet deep, coming from a never failing spring of pure crystal water, which is conveyed to the basin through a stone archway beneath the C.H.&D.* [Cincinnati, Hamilton and Dayton] *R.R. track, which supplies the brewery with the purest of spring water and also the ice used in summer.*

Years later, this picturesque hillside brewery would become the stage for an anti-Prohibition protest that would bring tears to the eyes of spectators.[54]

SCHMIDLAPPS AND SCHNEYERS

Ploch and his successors weren't Piqua's only source of beer. The Schneyer family was brewing at the south end of town, as was another family, the Schmidlapps.

William D. Schmidlapp (1839–1893) was working as a brewer by 1860, according to census records. His younger brother, Theodore (1845–1910), was in the business by 1866. Sons of Württemberg immigrant and pioneer grocer Jacob Adam Schmidlapp and his wife, Sophia Haug, the brothers were steeped in the local merchant trade—and, evidently, in the Noller sisters of Darke County.

Like Jacob Schmidlapp, Frederick Noller was an immigrant from Württemberg. Less is known about his wife, also named Sophia, but census records show they had several daughters. It isn't clear how the Schmidlapps got to know the Nollers, who lived twenty miles away in the Arcanum area. But William married three of them, starting in 1863, when he was twenty-three, with twenty-year-old Jacobine (1842–1864).

It must have been a shock to all when Jacobine died just a year later. William married again in 1865, this time choosing Jacobine's elder sister, Catharine (1840–1872), then about twenty-five. They had a son and a daughter in the seven years before she died. William waited two years before asking for the hand of twenty-two-year-old Elizabeth (1852–1926), the youngest of all. What fates befell her two sisters are unknown, but they didn't deter Elizabeth: she married William in 1874, bore two sons and lived to the age of seventy-four. She outlived William, who died at age fifty-three. In contrast to his brother, Theodore married just once, in 1873, to Caroline (1846–1927), yet another Noller sister.

Land records show William Schmidlapp and John L. Schneyer operated the old Weston brewery, at the southeast corner of Spring and Water, as Schmidlapp & Schneyer in 1862. Born in Saxony, Schneyer (1815–1882) was a generation older and had owned the old Weston site since 1851. At some point, Theodore Schmidlapp replaced Schneyer; Redfield and Logan's 1866 directory listed the brewery as Schmidlapp & Bro.

Karl Kaiser (or Kiser) (1840–1920), an immigrant from Baden, joined them in the 1870s. By 1879, William Schmidlapp and Kaiser were running the business as partners, with Theodore out of the picture. Their brewery sold 842 barrels in 1878 and 863 in 1879, according to Salem—about a third less than Butcher and Mittler.

But the partners were deep in debt. In June 1879, with a growing pile of bills and IOUs, they asked the county probate court to assign their property to Leopold Kiefer, a local businessman who had married the Schmidlapps' sister Emma two years earlier. Recognizing beer and brewing materials are perishable, the court allowed Kiefer to continue brewing to use up the remaining stock before disposing of the property.

This appears to have been the end of the Schmidlapps' brewery. William Schmidlapp kept the family home on the east side of the brewery until he

Lange's brewery workers gather outside the Spring Street Brewery, late 1800s. *Piqua Public Library.*

died in 1893, but lingering debt forced his widow, Elizabeth, to sell it in 1903. The Schmidlapp name endures in Piqua thanks to William's and Theodore's younger brother, Jacob G., who made a fortune as a Cincinnati banker and gave Piqua its first free public library, according to Jeff Suess's *Lost Cincinnati.*[55]

FIRE FRIDAY

Kaiser went on to a brewery on Ash Street between Spring and Harrison. The Ash Street Brewery earned its niche in history for an incident Rayner dubbed "Fire Friday."

Stephen Genslinger was a beloved fire chief who died at age fifty-four on September 29, 1885. On Friday, October 2, Genslinger's firefighters turned out with their horse-drawn fire wagons at his home on Water Street for the funeral service and a solemn procession to Forest Hill Cemetery. The cortège was about to get underway when Kaiser's brewery erupted in flames a block away. The firefighters had to leave their chief to go put out the fire. Afterward, they returned to finish the procession.

Kaiser's brewery survived the fire and made beer for more than ten years, but it was a small operation: The annual *Brewer's Guide* listed its output between 1,000 and 1,500 barrels in 1896, but it produced only 500 to 1,000 barrels in 1898. In 1899, an assignee for Kaiser sold the property. Records disclosed nothing more about the brewery or Kaiser.[56]

John L. Schneyer, meanwhile, opened a brewery sometime in the 1860s right across the street from the Schmidlapps, on the northeast corner of Spring and Water. Beers's *History of Miami County, Ohio* describes the brewery as a three-story building about sixty by eighty feet with a malting room, a cooling room, an icehouse and "extensive cellars." Schneyer's son, George (1846–1875), joined him as a partner. George died at about age twenty-nine, leaving his father to run the business until his own death in 1882.

CATHARINE SCHNEYER

John Schneyer's widow, Anna Catharine Waterman Schneyer (1828–1910), carried on the business with her children. Catharine had emigrated from Hanover in about 1834 and married John in 1845. She was another of the Miami Valley's women brewery proprietors who have gone unrecognized. For example, an 1890 issue of the *General Business Review of Miami County* didn't even name her in an article about the brewery: "One of the most prominent breweries in this section of the state is that of J.L. Schneyer. He is now deceased…but the business is carried on by his widow. Her son, C.L. Schneyer, is the general manager." The description implied Catharine was merely the owner of record, while her son did the real work. By this time, the two-story brick brewery had an annual capacity of six thousand barrels and employed five assistants.

Catharine and their children kept the brewery going until 1897, when the brothers Frank and Henry Lange entered the picture. Born in Minster, Frank (1858–1818) and Henry (1845–1909) were sons of Franz Lange, founder of Minster's Star Brewery. Frank was proprietor of Star Brewery for a short time between his father's retirement and its sale in 1883. Both brothers had moved to Grand Island, Nebraska, where they operated the Lange Brothers Brewery and sold "Golden Pilsner" beer. Eventually, they returned to the Miami Valley and bought the Schneyer brewery at the end of 1897.

Dry Vote, Wet Tears

By the turn of the twentieth century, Lange's and Schneider's were the only Piqua breweries still appearing in local records. A year before his death in 1903, Henry Schneider sold his brewery to Carl Schnell (1877–1932), the Ohio-born son of a saloonist from Germany.

But Schnell took over just as Prohibition was gaining power in Ohio. When the Rose law allowed Miami's electorate to vote the county dry in November 1908, he reacted the same way as Jacob Henne down in Troy—only with more theatrical flair. On January 22, 1909, his workers rolled out barrels of beer along the riverbank within sight of the Ash Street bridge. It was Schnell's entire stock—anywhere from 40 to 135 barrels, according to differing reports in the *Dayton Daily News* and beer journal *The Western Brewer*. They broke open the barrels one by one, dumping torrents of lager into the Great Miami. Legend has it bystanders on the bridge wept as the current carried the beer under their feet and down the river.

Carl Schnell's brewery, formerly Schneider's, about 1903. *Piqua Public Library.*

Lange Brewing Company's patriotically themed label. *Piqua Public Library.*

Frank Lange remained president of Lange Brewing until his death in 1918. That year, Frank N. (Nicholas) (1890–1952) and Fred J. (1893–1976), two of Frank's nine children, secured a bottling contract with Coca-Cola. Bottling soft drinks at Spring and Water Streets as the Lange Products Company kept the business alive through Prohibition. With its repeal in 1933, the company built a new bottling plant for Coke products on the northeast corner of the public square, on the site of the old Strand Theater building. The old plant briefly resumed beer production with the brands "Pioneer" and "Old Lager." Brewing ended in 1938 when the company converted the plant to ice and dairy products. By 1940, it was serving as a garage for the Coca-Cola operation, which continued for decades.[57]

SIDNEY

Sidney's history began nearly as early as Piqua's, ten miles up the Great Miami. But Sidney's brewing industry appears to have started much later than Piqua's and Dayton's, and it fell under the shadow of greater manufacturing accomplishments by the same family who started its first brewery.

Portrait of John Wagner. *From* History of Shelby County, Ohio.

The family name was Wagner, and numerous Wagner family members cofounded or were involved in the Wagner Manufacturing Company. Its cast aluminum and cast-iron cookware sold around the world and made Wagner a household name from the late 1800s through the first half of the twentieth century.

This line of Wagners descended from Mathias Wagner Sr. (1796–1841) and Marie Elizabeth Romons (1795–1868). They grew up in the Alsace region of northeastern France and came to America in 1830. They brought several children with them and added to the family after they reached Columbiana County in northeastern Ohio. The four sons connected with Sidney's brewing history were Mathias Jr. (1818–1888), Peter (1820–1908) and Joseph (or Anthony Joseph or Francis Joseph) (1821–1865), all born in Alsace; and John (circa 1834–1881), born in Columbiana County.

What drew them across the state isn't clear, but John C. Hover's *Memoirs of the Miami Valley* notes Joseph Wagner built a brewery in Sidney in 1850. County land records indicate it was a bit later: they show Francis Joseph Wagner and his wife, Josephine, bought property along the north side of East Poplar Street, between Miami Street and the river, from Philip and Magdalene Rauth for $3,000 in 1852. Joseph might have used the property earlier, but the records don't say. Either way, his brewery was the first of record in Sidney.

John Wagner leased the brewery from Joseph in 1859, according to Hover. Land records show Peter and John joined with another partner, Ferdinand (or Frederick) and Susannah Krebs, to buy the land in 1861 for $6,500. They sold their interest to Peter and John in 1865 for $2,500.

The business must have done well. John Wagner built an ornate Victorian house at 317 East Poplar Street in the mid-1860s. Decades before Mathias's sons, Milton and Bernard, would make Sidney known as the home of Wagner Manufacturing, the stately brick house spoke of the wealth Wagner beer had brought.

A Wagner Brewing building in 2018 was serving as a warehouse for Sidney City Schools. *Author's collection*.

Detail view of the Wagner Brewing building. *Author's collection*.

Few records could be found about the kinds of beers Peter and John Wagner produced from the 1860s until the mid-1870s, when they were operating as "Wagner & Bro." They appear to have been making common ales and porters. After John and his wife, Mary A., bought out Peter's interest in 1876 for $14,000, John "immediately began enlarging the works and preparing for the manufacture of lager beer," R. Sutton wrote in *History of Shelby County*. "Wagner's Golden Lager" became a popular brand, Sutton wrote. Later Wagner beer labels, bottle caps and signs also carried the names "Pale American Export," "Golden Pilsner" and "Triple XXX Sidney Beer."[58]

By 1880, John and Mary's sons had entered the business—Henry (1858–1935) as brewer and Edward (1860–1937) as bookkeeper. When John Wagner died in 1881, his sons carried on as John Wagner's Sons. They continued to expand and modernize. In 1893, they expanded their lagering cellars and ordered a thirty-five-ton refrigeration machine from W.P. Callahan & Company, a Dayton-based supplier to beer and commercial ice manufacturers across Ohio and in other states.[59]

John Wagner Sons and Mary A. Wagner

John Wagner's sons got credit for continuing the brewery, but another Wagner also deserves recognition: their mother, Mary. Born in Germany, Mary A. Myers (or Mayer) Wagner (1839–1918) was named president when the family incorporated the brewery as John Wagner Sons in November 1895. It was the same year Christina Schwind took the helm at Schwind Brewing in Dayton. Like Christina, Mary was an unsung trailblazer, the first woman brewery president in her county, but barely mentioned in local history books. Under her, Henry was vice-president and Edward secretary-treasurer. The arrangement raises the question of whether Mary had been playing some role, if not already running the business, for the fourteen years since John's death—and what role she might have played in his shadow. Mary remained president until about age seventy-five, when she appeared with that title in the 1914 *American Brewers' Review*; its 1915 issue listed Henry as president and another son, Louis F. (1866–1952), as vice-president.[60]

Production grew through the end of the century. The 1896 *Brewer's Guide* listed John Wagner Sons' yearly output at ten to twelve thousand barrels. Two years later, production grew to twelve to fourteen thousand barrels. The

Top: Bottle caps from the John Wagner Company on display at the Shelby County Historical Society. *Author's collection.*

Bottom: Small sign advertising Wagner's Pale American beverage on display at the Shelby County Historical Society. *Author's collection.*

company continued to invest in new equipment, including a bottling plant in the winter of 1911–12.

John Wagner Sons' brewery stood alone in Shelby County, so it dominated the local beer market. At the same time, the perishable nature of the product meant the brewery couldn't ship its beer far, so it depended on local sales. To keep growing, wrote Richard H. Wallace in *Voices from the Past*, the company "concentrated its efforts on increasing consumption. Free lunches, gambling and other enticements kept the men (and some women) coming to the bars on a regular basis. Beer had surpassed distilled spirits as the main source of alcohol in America by 1890, and that was also the case in Sidney."

Not everyone loved the saloons. Local women formed the Women's Temperance League of Sidney in 1874, the year of the temperance crusade, and set up a chapter of the Woman's Christian Temperance Union in 1890. They campaigned to ban alcoholic beverage sales in 1908. But county voters in 1908 chose to keep Shelby wet even as many counties around it, including neighboring Miami, went dry. Open saloons in nearby Sidney inflamed anti-liquor passions in Piqua. Dr. William E. Biederwolf of the Piqua Ministerial Association, leader of the local temperance movement, reflected local outrage and frustration, according to Wallace. In a 1911 speech, he said, "We gave the devil the best run for his money he ever had. We ran him out of this county into… Sidney, his headquarters."

The upshot was Wagner's brewery started the new century with more business than ever. By 1913, Hitchcock wrote, "Their present plant covers an acre of ground, is equipped with the latest and best cooling machinery, with storage cellars that have a capacity of 28,000 barrels. Their annual output exceeds 24,000 barrels of the Golden Pilsner Lager and the bottled Pale American Export."

But Shelby County couldn't vote down the Eighteenth Amendment in 1919 or Ohio's own prohibition amendment, which took effect in May 1919. The impact on brewers like John Wagner Sons was immediate. "Following example set by many other manufactories of its class, the plant has been converted to the production of a 'soft drink' and will hereafter be known as 'The Wagner Beverage Company,'" noted *Memoirs of the Miami Valley*, published that year. Land records show the Wagners dissolved the John Wagner Sons Brewing Company that same year and distributed its assets to John and Mary Wagner's children, who were also the company's stockholders.

Prohibition might have been only one factor in the decision to break up the company. It also followed Mary A. Wagner's death the year before.

The Twenty-First Amendment repealed Prohibition at the end of 1933. Sidney's brewery reincorporated in 1935 as the John Wagner Company. Edward Wagner, who had become owner of the brewery lots, sold them to the company for $10,000. Edward's sons ran the company—Carl (or Karl) J. was president and George E. was secretary. But it didn't last. Land records show the company went bankrupt in 1941, and a receiver auctioned the company's assets for $16,000.

John Wagner's house still stands near the brewery site on Poplar Street. In 2018, it was owned by the Aspen Family Center. *Author's collection.*

The company is gone, but as of this writing, a long brick building once a part of the brewery still stands on East Poplar; Sidney City Schools uses it for storage. John Wagner's house also stands, preserved as the Aspen Family Center, a mental health facility.[61]

CHAPTER 6

AUGLAIZE COUNTY

LAND OF THE WOODEN SHOE

The route of the Miami and Erie Canal follows the Great Miami River northward from Dayton, but above Piqua it veers northwest, cutting across a patchwork quilt of farmland toward St. Marys and the Loramie Summit—a flat area where the canal reaches its highest point, 512 feet above the Ohio River and 395 feet above Lake Erie. The region's largest geographical feature, the twelve-thousand-acre Grand Lake, was dug between 1837 and 1845 as a reservoir to feed the canal. As of this writing, some sections of the canal are preserved and the reservoir functions as a shallow recreational lake.[62]

The canal was a water highway for immigrants who settled in the Miami Valley's northern counties beginning in the early 1800s. The area around Grand Lake, especially to the south, is known as the "Land of the Cross Tipped Churches" because of the many Catholic churches built by German immigrants. Several towns reflect their German heritage with names such as Maria Stein, Minster and New Bremen in Auglaize and Mercer Counties.

One might expect to find hometown breweries as an expression of German culture, at least in the larger communities of Piqua, Sidney, Wapakoneta and Greenville. But they have none as of this writing, although one was nearing completion in Troy. Oddly, the only craft breweries close enough to be called local are in the most sparsely populated areas.

Nick Moeller, founder-owner of Moeller Brew Barn. *Author's collection.*

NO SUBMARINES IN MARIA STEIN

One is the Moeller Brew Barn in Mercer County, just north of Maria Stein, a village of about two thousand people some six miles west of Minster. Moeller, a Maria Stein native, opened the brewery in 2015 with his wife, Monica, because…well, there weren't any submarines in Maria Stein.

Moeller spent much of his earlier adult life in San Diego, where he maintained navy submarines as a civilian engineer at the Portsmouth Naval Shipyard. He and Monica, who was from Burbank, Washington, decided to raise their children in Moeller's hometown. But Nick had developed a passion for brewing in San Diego, so he decided to launch a new career in Maria Stein by building a craft brewery. "What was I going to do for a living? There's no submarines there," he said in 2017.

The brewery sold about 1,100 barrels that year, but in 2019 Moeller completed a major addition that added a kitchen and greatly expanded production. As if this writing, Moeller beer is sold across the region. The beers reflect local geography and culture. Sawcreek Pale took its name from nearby Chickasaw Creek. Blackberry Prairie Wheat uses fruit from the farm of a neighbor who suggested the recipe. And Wally Post Red is named for a Major League Baseball player from Mercer County.[63]

Franz Joseph Stallo

A century and a half ago, small breweries were common in the budding towns of the Miami Valley. Immigrants coming to the New World from England, France, Ireland and the German states weren't about to leave behind their beer—especially Germans, who began pouring into the upper Miami Valley early in the nineteenth century.

Like other immigrant groups, Germans often faced hostility and discrimination from more established populations. An infamous example in Cincinnati was the April 1855 attack by an anti-immigration mob against the Over-the-Rhine area. German residents formed a militia and barricaded Vine Street, fighting off the mob for three days. Not surprisingly, Germans tended to stick together as they moved up the Miami Valley.[64]

Minster is a classic example of a tight-knit community built by German immigrants on the Ohio frontier. A village of about 2,800 people as of this writing, it retains much of its German character. The twin-steepled St. Augustine Catholic Church, a Gothic Revivalist cathedral on Hanover Street, remains the village's most prominent architectural landmark since immigrants built its first walls in 1848. And tiny Minster would become the home of a powerhouse brewery whose flagship brand was known around the country.

Its story starts with Franz Joseph Stallo (1793–1833) of Sierhausen, Parish of Damme, in the southern part of the Grand Duchy of Oldenburg, later in Lower Saxony in northwestern Germany. Stallo was at the forefront of a great migration of frustrated German reformers. A printer, bookbinder and publisher who also studied horticulture and electricity, Stallo nettled Oldenburg authorities with rebellious tracts and

St. Augustine Catholic Church, Minster. *Author's collection.*

songs that also advocated emigration. By one account—Clifford Neal Smith's *Early Nineteenth-Century German Settlers in Ohio*—they jailed him for several months in early 1831.

Once released, Stallo took his own advice and headed for America. He left in April 1831 with five children and an ailing wife, who died in Amsterdam as they waited to sail. The widower Stallo, his children and a nurse arrived in New York in June and reached Cincinnati in July. He found a job in a print shop and began sending letters back home about the wonders of Ohio. Some of his letters were published, and they sparked a local emigration movement. Many joined Stallo in Cincinnati.

Like Stallo, most of the immigrants from his area were Roman Catholic. They found themselves less than welcome in Cincinnati, where native-born Protestants were in the majority and wanted to keep it that way. Stallo pushed the idea among his friends of building their own community in the wilderness up north. In September 1832, a group of young immigrants formed a stock company. They charged Stallo and six other men with finding a townsite and buying the land.

Stallo's group went up the Miami to a U.S. government land office in Piqua or Sidney (accounts differ) and found a site about fourteen miles northwest of Sidney. It lay on a trail long used by native people, British traders and army forces. The Miami and Erie Canal didn't yet reach Piqua, but Stallo may have learned it would eventually pass near their site. Deal done, they went back to Cincinnati to share the news. The group discussed what to name their new home, finally settling on Stallostown. It probably didn't hurt that, at least by Smith's account, Stallo provided a barrel of beer for the occasion.

Settlers started moving in immediately, cutting a clearing in the great oak forest covering the land. More than one hundred settlers occupied Stallostown by the summer of 1833, with more on the way.

An outbreak of cholera swept through the Ohio region that summer, killing more than thirty in Stallostown alone, including Stallo. But the survivors persevered. The Catholic Church established a mission in 1834, and the settlers built a large log church in 1835. Their fledgling mission became St. Augustine Parish in 1836, and the town briefly took the name Münster—a German word for church or cathedral—before changing it to Minster.

PIONEER BREWERS

For Minster's settlers, life on the frontier didn't mean life without beer. Louis, Rita and David Hoying's parish history *Pilgrims All: A History of Saint Augustine Parish* describes the use of beer and wine in local harvest and wedding festivities, including consequences for *not* providing it: "If the bridegroom did not offer to treat his fellow youths the evening before the wedding to a draught of beer, they would build, during the night, enormous hay stacks before the entrance of his home, thus hindering his exit in the morning."

Minster's population would seem to have been too small in the early 1800s to support a commercial brewery. Another cholera outbreak in 1849 killed 250, about a quarter of the village. Its population was only about 1,100 by 1890, according to the U.S. Census. But the 1850 census identified three residents as brewers: Garrett Lukmann (1806–1860); his fifteen-year-old son, Ferdinand; and Frederick Myer, a seventeen-year-old who lived with them. *W.W. Reilly & Co.'s Ohio State Business Directory*

THE STAR BREWING Co., Minster, Ohio

A 1907 postcard illustration of the Star Brewery. *Minster Historical Society and Museum.*

for 1853–4 lists "John G. Luckmann" as a brewer in Minster. Census and cemetery records suggest Garrett and John G. both referred to Johann Gerhard Luckmann, who was born in Germany in 1806, died in 1860 and is buried at St. Augustine Catholic Cemetery. Ferdinand Luckman is the only Minster brewer listed in a business directory on the 1860s *Map of Auglaize County*. The 1870 census lists Ferdinand and a younger brother, August, as brewers. This was the latest record we found that mentioned Luckman's brewery. The 1880 census suggests it may have closed sometime in the 1870s, as it lists Ferdinand as a teamster and August as working in a boot and shoe factory.[65]

STAR BREWING

The Star Brewery was the legacy of Franz (or Frank) Lange (1822–1907). He was born in Baden, later a part of the state of Baden-Württemberg in southwestern Germany. He farmed until deciding to start a brewery in 1869. The 1935 *Lima News* reported the original plant was a two-story brick building that stood on the west side of Ohio Street south of Third, a block west of the Miami and Erie Canal. Lange initially used horsepower to grind malt and pump water, but he soon replaced it with a steam engine. The 1880 *Atlas of Auglaize County* reported Lange spent $40,000 to build the brewery and was adding $15,000 worth of improvements in 1880.

The brewery's first years of sales are unknown, but Salem's 1880 *Beer, Its History and Its Economic Value as a National Beverage* reported sales of 1,790 barrels in 1878 and 2,144 barrels in 1879. Two of Lange's children, Frank Jr. and Henry, had a hand in the brewery until they moved to Nebraska, where they started a brewery in Grand Island before returning to Ohio to buy the Schneyer Brewery in Piqua.

Numerous published accounts credit Lange as the first to produce lager beer in Minster. Under the label "Wooden Shoe Beer," it became popular in town and surrounding communities. Lange sold the business in 1883 to Theodore B. and Charles Steineman, sons of Minster pioneer John Henry Steinemann. Both Minster natives, Theodore (1839–1922) and Charles (1847–1928) kept the business going well enough to rebuild immediately when a fire burned the brewery to the ground in 1888.

Frank Herkenhoff bought into the business in 1890 and operated it with three partners—Matthias Goeke, A.W. Gerwals and Bernard Frierott, who

Brewery of Steinemann & Bro.

Steinemann Brothers Brewery in Minster. *Minster Historical Society and Museum.*

became brewery manager. Herkenhoff (1838–1918) was a first-generation Minster native who moved among coopering jobs in Minster, Cincinnati and Tippecanoe before settling in Minster to run his own cooperage. Herkenhoff sold his business to his employees in 1890 to join the brewery. He went on to become its president. Herkenhoff apparently enjoyed a long, healthy life, remaining active until he collapsed and died without warning less than two months before his eightieth birthday, according to his obituary in the *Minster Post.*

Frierott (1854–1903) also was a lifelong Minster resident. During his tenure, the brewery expanded and modernized with a refrigeration system in 1890, a bottling line in 1892 and an ice-making plant in 1901, among other improvements. It was selling between six and seven thousand barrels of lager per year by 1896, according to that year's *Brewer's Guide.*

Frierott managed the brewery until his death in 1903. At that time, the company's directors reorganized the business as Star Brewing Company with Goeke as president; Frank Herkenhoff as vice-president; Frank's son, Charles, as manager; and A.W. Gerwels and George Van Oss as

Undated drawing of Wooden Shoe Brewing. *Minster Historical Society and Museum.*

directors. Van Oss retired from the business in 1907, succeeded by Anton W. Frierott (1885–1956), a son of Bernard. (How long Goeke served as president is unknown; the 1910 census, a year before his death, lists his occupation as "none.")

Charles Herkenhoff (1864–1928) attended St. Mary's College (now the University of Dayton) and owned a retail store before joining Star Brewing. In his time there, eventually as president, output grew to sixteen thousand barrels per year. With the ratification of the Eighteenth Amendment in 1919, the company changed its name to the Star Beverage Company, and production switched from the company's popular Wooden Shoe lager to near beer and sodas.

When Charles Herkenhoff died in 1928, the directors appointed Anton to succeed him. Anton took over the company eight years after the onset of Prohibition and just in time for the Great Depression. Fortunately, he had the help of a brewmaster who was a local legend.[66]

THE BREWMASTERS

More than other communities, Minster revered its brewmasters. The brewmasters refined their beer with selected ingredients—including malt from as far as Wisconsin and hops from the old country. A 1909 *Minster Post* article (as recounted in a later report) boasted that "Minster beer is one of the few American beers that one can drink without experiencing headache and other hangovers." Over the course of Star Brewing's history, two brewmasters were responsible for nearly all of its beer.

The first was Peter H. Mittler (1841–1925), a native of Frimmersdorf, Germany. Born in 1841, he immigrated to America in 1868. Features about the brewery in a 1935 *Lima News* and a 1939 *Minster Post* both reported Lange hired Mittler in 1870, soon after he had started his brewery. Some later accounts give the same year. But they don't square with Mittler family census, marriage, birth, death and cemetery records that indicate Mittler was a brewer in Cincinnati and Newport, Kentucky, in the early 1870s before coming to Minster, possibly by way of Piqua at the end of the decade.

Cincinnati directories show a Peter Mittler working as a brewer for Christian Moerlein in 1870. In 1872, he was across the Ohio River in Newport, Kentucky, where he married Eleanora Anna Christmann. Census and marriage records show they had three children: Bertha and Clara, both born in Newport in 1875 and 1877, and Cecilia, born in 1878 in an undetermined place. The 1872 Newport directory listed Mittler as a maltster working for Johann Butscher and George Wiedemann's brewery. Butscher's son, John Butcher, drove a wagon for it.

Directories for the next two years found Mittler back in Cincinnati, working as a brewer for an unnamed brewery. No later records of him in Cincinnati were found, but Miami County land records show Hartman Ploch, in September 1879, leased his brewery to John Butcher Jr. and Peter Mittler. And a brewer with a poorly written name indexed as "P.A. Midler" appears in the 1880 census for Piqua, with a wife and children of the same names, ages and birthplaces. They were living next door to Ploch.

No names similar to Peter Mittler appear in the 1870 census for Minster and the surrounding Jackson Township. Strangely, he *does* appear in the 1880 census for Minster, along with the same family members as in Piqua. This Peter Mittler was also a brewer, living next to Lange. Both census sheets were dated in June of that year. The nearly identical records are a mystery unless one assumes Mittler happened to move his family from Piqua to Minster while the census was underway and let himself be counted twice.

Left: Peter Mittler, Star Brewing's first brewmaster. *Minster Historical Society and Museum.*

Right: Joseph Brinkman, Minster's brewmaster for fifty-five years. *Minster Historical Society and Museum.*

Mittler's timeline from 1880 is more straightforward. Cecilia Mittler died in Minster in October 1880. Her mother, Eleanora, died a month later. Peter married Elisabeth Menkhaus (1862–1913) a year later and had five children with her. He served as brewmaster until 1890 but was a member of the new company that bought the brewery from the Steinmann brothers in 1890. Accounts differ about how long he remained with the company. The 1900 census for Minster listed him as a "capitalist," but by 1910 he was a boot and shoe merchant in Delphos, about thirty miles north. He died there in 1925.

Mittler didn't leave Minster high and dry when he stepped down. Another brewmaster was waiting in the wings—or, more precisely, the cellars.

Joseph Brinkman (1865–1943) emigrated from the Prussian province of Westphalia (now the western German state of North Rhine–Westphalia) in 1883. Like Mittler, he spent a year in Newport before settling in Minster. He took a job as a cellarman at Star Brewing in 1884, charged with ensuring the stored beer kept its quality. Mittler's departure five years later gave Brinkman the chance to step up, but first he sharpened his brewing skills by attending the American Brewing

Academy in Chicago. Returning after a year, he assumed the title of brewmaster and held it for fifty-five years, until his death at age seventy-eight. An obituary in the *Minster Post* reported he was "affectionately known to practically everyone in this community."

Prohibition must have been a dark time for Brinkman. "Altho he remained with the plant, Brinkman said that he watched restlessly" for it to end, the 1935 *Lima News* reported.[67]

THE WOODEN SHOE

Despite the Depression, Star Brewing poured $200,000 into the operation. It modernized the plant, added a rathskeller and spruced up the grounds with landscaping and an ornamental pond. Shipping beer as far as Florida and New York, the brewery set an all-time record of 135,000 barrels in 1935, the 1939 *Minster Post* reported. The village clerk that year said Wooden Shoe's beer taxes and liquor permit fees covered all of Minster's operating expenses from 1935 through 1937. With the fame of its flagship beer spreading, Star Brewing changed its name in 1939 to Wooden Shoe Brewing.

Anton W. Frierott led the brewery out of Prohibition and through the Depression. The brewery was roaring by 1939, but 1940 opened with a personal tragedy for Frierott. His youngest brother, Bernard H., manager of the brewery's bottling department, was at work two days before Christmas when he suddenly fell ill. He was diagnosed with heart disease and died at home twenty-three days later. He was thirty-eight. He left behind a widow and two sons, including one born four days before his death. Anton retired later in 1941.

The Wooden Shoe Brewing Company survived Prohibition and the Great Depression, but it couldn't compete as the beer industry consolidated around national brands. A Chicago syndicate bought the business in 1946. Sales declined, and the company fell into receivership in 1953.

The old brewery served as a warehouse for years. The Minster Canning Company occupied it beginning in 1964, and in 1967, it bought the building and the 11.5-acre parcel on which it stood. Eventually, a local metal processing startup, Precision Strip Inc., bought the property and razed the remaining buildings.[68]

The brand enjoyed a brief revival between 2005 and 2012. Andy Philpot and his parents, Gene and Mary Lou, formed the Wooden Shoe Brewing

Trucks at Star Brewing, early 1900s. *From the* Atlas and History of Auglaize County *(1917).*

Company LLC and served samples of a trial brew at the 2006 Minster Oktoberfest. They opened a microbrewery in a converted storage building at 69 South Garfield Street in 2010, producing lager, bock and a Belgian-style wheat beer dubbed Stallostown. But the brewery closed in August 2012.

Records of old breweries leave few clues about the flavor of the beers they produced. Wooden Shoe is a rare exception: its legacy lives on in a national brand with roots in the company.

Wooden Shoe's last brewmaster was Charles Koch (1922–2011), a Cincinnati native, chemist and fifth-generation brewer. He graduated from Chicago's Siebel Institute of Technology, America's oldest brewing school, in 1948. He worked in Cincinnati breweries before becoming Wooden Shoe's brewmaster in the early 1950s. After it closed, he returned to Cincinnati for a career as a chemist. But in his attic he kept a trunk of old family brewing memorabilia, including recipes from the 1800s.

In 1984, Koch's son, Jim, caught the brewing bug. He had studied business at Harvard and was living in Boston, but he found the old recipe, tested it in his kitchen and took it to market as Samuel Adams Boston Lager, named for one of America's founding fathers. It became the flagship beverage of Koch's Boston Beer Company, which helped trigger the rebirth of craft beer in America.[69]

NEW BREMEN

New Bremen's history began much like Minster's. It started with German immigrants in Cincinnati who formed a stock company in 1832. The next year, they laid out their town right on the path of the future Miami and Erie Canal, immediately north of Minster. New Bremen stood at the point where the canal began its long, barely perceptible fall to Lake Erie. It became the home of the canal's Lock One North. As of this writing, New Bremen is a village of about three thousand people and the home of international forklift maker Crown Equipment. But New Bremen still treasures its canal heritage: the town seal depicts a canalboat between the gates of the lock, and it is the home of the Miami and Erie Canal Corridor Association.

Unlike Minster, New Bremen's settlers were mainly Protestant. Also unlike Minster, New Bremen supported not one but two hometown breweries in the 1860s, according to the 1860s *Map of Auglaize County*. It places them just a block apart on the east side of North Main Street, midway on the blocks north and south of Second.

One brewery acquired a notoriety now a part of local folklore. In the late 1870s, the Meyer and Schwers Brewery was situated on what later became residential properties at 212 and 214 North Main. The New Bremen Historic Association identified the business as "Henry Schwer's saloon," but other sources labeled it as a small brewery. It might have been both. As the story goes, sometime in the early 1880s, Schwers (1838–1899) refused to serve a customer who came in already besotted. Schwers drew the customer's ire, and the customer drew a pistol. A .22-caliber bullet went into Schwers's mouth behind his jaw, and his teeth stopped it. Schwers spat the bullet onto the floor. The customer went to prison, the bullet became a family heirloom and Schwers became a minor legend.

The histories of the two breweries are murky. The 1860s Auglaize map marked breweries at both locations. Land records show both lots— Lot 22 north of Second, Lot 28 south—were owned in the 1850s by a Frederick Kohlhorst. A sudden jump in the property values at that time suggests Kohlhorst might have built a brewery on one or both lots. But numerous Kohlhorsts lived in the area, and the handwritten land, census and other records often used different given names and various spellings of surnames. New Bremen's first brewer evaded positive identification.

What the records do show is a succession of brewers and saloon keepers in the ensuing years. The west half of Lot 28, midway between First and Second, went to Fredrick I. (or F.I., or F.J.) Steinberg in 1870. Steinberg sold

The Miami and Erie Canal's restored Lock One in New Bremen. *Author's collection.*

it to his brother, Adolf, in 1881. Adolf sold it in 1894, by which time he was living in Wapakoneta and running the Steinberg Hotel. No proof surfaced that either brother had a brewery on the premises. Adolf appears in the 1880 census as a saloon keeper and Fredrick as a merchant.

There's more information about brewing on Lot 22, north of Second, where Schwers had his business. It saw a series of owners after Kohlhorst. A.F. William (or William A.F.) Meyer bought the property for $1,000 in 1860, and the 1860s Auglaize map lists him as a brewer. In 1866, he sold it to Michael Vossler, Christian Kah and Christian Fischer for nine times the 1860 price. That same year, Fischer sold out to the other two partners, and then Kah sold his share to Peter Wagner. Wagner sold his share to Vossler the next year, and Vossler took on Ernst Henry (or Heinrich) Lameyer as a partner until 1870, when Lameyer sold his share back to Vossler.

Vossler's brewery must have faced growing competition in the 1870s as the Star Brewery's business flourished less than four miles down the canal. The 1870 industry census put the Vossler-Lameyer brewery's production at 425 barrels. In 1877, Vossler fell into insolvency, and his property went to Herman E. Meyer and Henry Schwers in a sheriff's sale. Salem reported Meyer and Schwers sold 320 barrels in 1878—down by a fourth. It isn't clear when the brewing ended, but the 1880 census lists Meyer as a saloon keeper, and he sold his share of the brewery lot to Schwers in 1882.

The New Bremen Historic Association, 120 North Main Street, stands two lots north of where an 1860s map showed an early brewery stood. *Author's collection.*

After Schwers died in 1899, his widow, Anna, married Joseph Drexler. In 1907, they turned over the property to Henry and Anna's daughter, Amelia Schwers, who eventually sold it in four parcels. But with Star Brewing going gangbusters next door in Minster, it's unlikely New Bremen's beer drinkers suffered.[70]

WAPAKONETA

A town of just under ten thousand at the 2010 census, Wapakoneta is the seat of Auglaize County's government and home to the Armstrong Air and Space Museum. The museum honors the memory of Wapakoneta's most famous son, Neil A. Armstrong, who made the first footprints on the moon in 1969.

But what about Kolter and Koch? They were prominent names in their times, associated with the City Beer Company and Old Vienna Beer. But unlike Armstrong, Kolter and Koch didn't have the whole world watching when they made their first small steps for beer, and few remembered them by the twenty-first century.

CHARLES KOLTER

Charles Kolter (1832–1905) was a native of Rhine Province, Bavaria, according to a biographical sketch in the 1898 *Atlas of Auglaize County*. A son of Karl Kolter, he emigrated at age nineteen and lived in several places before settling in Wapakoneta. He worked as a blacksmith and bought an interest in the Home Milling Company. In 1862, he bought land for a brewery with three other men: Lewis Kolter, Henry Frech and Zachariah Meng. They paid $250, or $62.50 apiece if they anted up equally. The brewery stood on the east side of North Water Street, north of North Street and close to a tight bend in the Auglaize River. A self-storage facility stands there as of this writing.

Records indicate Meng was in charge. The 1860s Auglaize map labeled the brewery as Meng's, and the deed transfer record of Lewis Kolter's sale in 1865 identified the brewery "as doing business under the name and style of Meng & Co." But they say little about Meng himself except

he was born in Württemberg in about 1837 and married another Württemberg native, Anna Schragle, in 1861. *Williams' Ohio State Directory for 1872–1873* shows him with a saloon on Auglaize Street.

Kolter bought out his partners over the next few years. William, his younger brother, bought a share in 1868, and they operated as "C. Kolter and Brother." The 1870 industrial census lists it as a lager beer brewery with three employees and a capital investment of $10,000. Salem reported it sold 1,049 barrels in 1878 and 1,149 barrels in 1879. The 1880 atlas identifies the Kolter brewery as "William Kolter & Bro," but William sold his share that same year.[71]

Portrait of Charles Kolter. *From the* Atlas of Auglaize County *(1898).*

HENRY KOCH

In 1880, Henry Koch was on his way to becoming a wagon maker. He was a twenty-year-old apprentice to his father, Jacob. But in September 1882, he married Charles Kolter's daughter, Caroline Elizabeth. Sometime in the 1880s, Kolter's brewery changed from Kolter & Bro. to Kolter & Koch. Sanborn insurance maps depict steady growth toward the end of the century—by 1885, the brewery included a malt room and icehouse, and by 1892, it had a bottling works on the west side of Water Street. The maps also called it "Kolter and Koch City Brewery" by then. The brewery sold between three and four thousand barrels of lager in 1898, according to that year's *Brewer's Guide*, which identified it simply as the City Brewing Company.

In 1901, four years before his death, Charles sold the brewery to Koch and his son, Charles T. Kolter (1857–1941), Caroline's elder brother. The business continued to prosper with the second generation in charge. "The output is sufficient to supply the demands of a large extent of territory. Two large ice machines are also operated in connection with

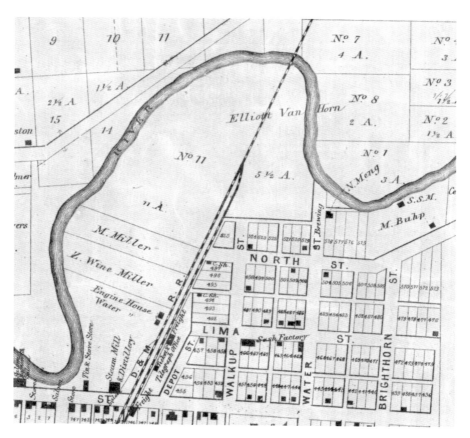

This 1860s map labels the location of Wapakoneta's first known brewery as "N. Meng." *Map of Auglaize County, Ohio.*

the brewery. The larger ice machine producing fifty tons per day and the smaller one twenty tons per day," according to C.W. Williamson in *History of Western Ohio and Auglaize County*.

The onset of statewide prohibition in 1919 and looming national Prohibition must have caused a sea change in City Brewing's operations. Charles T. deeded his share of the business to Henry and Caroline in 1921. That same year, the trade press reported the incorporation of the Koch Beverage and Ice Company.

The reorganization put a new generation in charge. Henry and Caroline's son Karl was president. Carl Siferd, who had married their daughter Cora, was vice-president. Other members of the Koch family also held officer positions.

The Kochs steered the company through the Prohibition era, selling soft drinks and ice. Karl's son, George Henry, took over in later years, doing business as the Koch Beverage Company and Koch Beverage and Ice. It sold Old Vienna English Style Ale in the 1930s and '40s before it, like so many others, fell under the wheels of national brands.

Koch's was the last brewery in Wapakoneta as of this writing, but it wasn't the first of record. The 1860s Auglaize map shows another brewery standing on the south side of Benton between Broadway and Seltzer, about two miles south of City Brewing. Its proprietor was Leopold Jacobs (1824–1902), one of Wapakoneta's early brewers.[72]

LEOPOLD JACOBS

Born in Bavaria, Jacobs immigrated to America in 1848—just in time to serve in the Mexican-American War, according to his obituary in the Lima, Ohio *Times-Democrat*. He worked in the California gold fields until 1852, married a sixteen-year-old French immigrant named Theresia Melchior and moved to Wapakoneta in 1858. The 1860 census identified him as a brewer two years before Kolter, Frech and Meng are known to have started brewing. His brewery was producing five hundred barrels per year by 1870, according to that year's industrial census.

Anecdotal evidence suggests two brothers, Louis Schuman (1846–1880) and George Schuman (1850–1933), took over the brewery from Jacobs after at least one, Louis, apprenticed with him. The clues are scattered through census records and business directories. The 1860 census shows a Lewis

PLANT OF CITY BREWING CO., WAPAKONETA

City Brewing Company plant in Wapakoneta. *From the* Atlas and History of Auglaize County *(1917)*.

Schuman, thirteen, and George, ten, both born in New York, in the care of a governess from Bavaria named Catharine Oart. The 1870 census has a Louis Schuman of corresponding age boarding with Jacobs. The 1880 atlas shows a brewery next to Jacobs's property with "L. and G. Schuman" and lists "Gorge Schuman & Bro." as brewers in its business directory. The 1880 census identifies "Ludwig" and George Schuman as brewers. It doesn't show their relationship, but they were of corresponding ages, lived close together and claimed Germany as their parents' homeland.

A generation older than the Schumans, Jacobs might have made them apprentices and later successors to his brewery. If so, the brewery declined on their watch. Salem reported they sold 278 and 300 barrels in 1878 and 1879, less than a third of the Kolter brewery's sales in the same period and half of what Jacobs produced in 1870.

One reason why they sold so much less than Kolter might have been their product. While the Kolters were brewing lager, the Schumans were "brewers of common beer," according to the 1880 atlas. What happened to the Schuman brewery isn't clear, but Louis Schuman died in 1880 at about age thirty-four. The 1900 census found George working as a janitor. Louis is buried at St. Joseph Cemetery under the name "Schuman," while George, who lived another fifty-three years, is interred at Greenlawn as "Schumann."[73]

CHAPTER 7

RAILROADS AND BEER IN DARKE COUNTY

Twenty miles north of Greenville on Ohio Route 118, a dairy barn built in 1933 makes a picturesque gateway to the village of Coldwater in Mercer County. In 2015, the vacant dairy saw new life as the home of Tailspin Brewing.

While the building outwardly mirrors the area's rural character, its new owner chose to decorate the interior in an aviation theme. Pictures of airplanes adorn the taproom. Every pint glass has a propeller etched on it. The aerial theme reflects owner and founder Jack Waite's years as a U.S. Air Force officer and fighter pilot. He picked up the homebrewing hobby during his military career. When he retired, he wanted a new challenge and decided to open a brewpub.

Twenty miles from the nearest city seems like an odd place to open as intensely local a business as a brewpub, but Waite's small-business model fit the market. He was brewing six hundred to seven hundred barrels per year in 2018. "I sell seven barrels in a weekend, so I don't have to go far to sell what I make. I intend to focus on this barn and keep it small," he said.

Village breweries used to dot the Miami Valley. Waite found it was still the norm in southwestern Germany, where he was stationed in the mid-1990s. "Every little village had their own brewery, and that was their brewery, so they frequented that brewery. That's very much the way Coldwater and the surrounding area has gotten their arms around us," Waite said. At the same time, he found some business coming from out of town: "There's a lot of folks out there that do beer tourism on the weekend."[74]

Jack Waite, owner of Tailspin Brewing. *Author's collection.*

GREENVILLE

Greenville is known as the hometown of Annie Oakley and a Whirlpool KitchenAid plant. It's Darke County's seat of government and the biggest city in Darke, Mercer or Preble Counties in western Ohio. But as of this writing, only three brewpubs were closer than a thirty-minute drive: Tailspin, Moeller Brew Barn in Maria Stein and Hairless Hare Brewery in Vandalia—each about twenty miles distant.

It wasn't always so. For more than a century, small breweries were common. In Darke County, they clustered in Greenville, but Union City and even tiny New Madison had them.

Greenville was the setting of a pivotal episode in Ohio's—and the nation's—history as the site of the Treaty of Greenville of 1795. Just eight years after the treaty signing, Ohio became the seventeenth state. Greenville became a village in 1808.

This section about Greenville's brewing history greatly benefits from the work of Jeff Puterbaugh, a local breweriana collector who shared his carefully documented research. He tracked down the earliest records of a commercial brewery in Greenville.[75]

It opened for business around 1851 at 142 West Water Street, close to Greenville Creek. This is when Albert Lehmkuhl (born in 1825), a German immigrant, bought a lot there; the 1850 census identifies him as a brewer.

Lehmkuhl sold the part of the lot containing the brewery a year later to two men who, in turn, sold their portions to Joseph Katzenberger (1828–1884). The 1857 *Map of Darke County* identifies the brewery as Katzenberger's. An immigrant from what was then the Grand Duchy of Baden, Katzenberger, his brothers and their father were involved in the failed German revolution of 1848, according to W.H. McIntosh's *History of Darke County*. They immigrated to America in 1850. Joseph bought a share of the brewery in 1852, and he became sole owner two years later. His brother Charles joined him in the business in 1861, and they operated it until 1868, when they sold it to Michael Weinbrecht and Michael Steinhelber (or Steinhilber).

Weinbrecht sold his half interest to Steinhelber just two years later. Steinhelber ran the business himself for two years before picking up a new partner, Jacob Maybrun. An ever-rising price for the property suggests the business was thriving: Steinhelber had paid Weinbrecht $5,000 for his half interest, but Maybrun paid $7,500. When Maybrun sold out to John F. Reinhardt in 1874, he collected $9,000.

The business became Reinhardt-Steinhelber, but Steinhelber didn't seem to like the arrangement. Just a year later, he petitioned the county court to dissolve the partnership. A new investor, Charles Bachman, picked up Reinhardt's half interest for $9,000 in December 1875, and the next month he bid $10,506 for Steinhelber's share in a public auction. It isn't clear what happened to the business over the next year and a half, but Bachman sold it all in August 1877 for just $12,295—a huge loss.

The new owner was German immigrant Detrick Glander (1818–1902). He quickly ran into debt and had to sell everything he owned to satisfy creditors. Appraised at $10,000, the brewery found no takers until 1882, when it was reappraised at $4,000 and Bachman's wife, Julia, bought it at that price. The Bachmans immediately resold it to George and Edward Glander, sons of Detrick. They paid $5,000 for the brewery and another $2,700 on a note Julia Bachman had given to the Darke County sheriff.

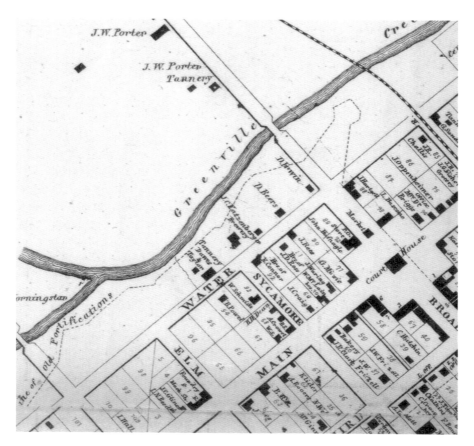

Location of Joseph Katzenberger's brewery in Greenville. *Map of Darke County (1857).*

The brewery didn't stay idle all that time. A man named Chris Jenney ran the beer business in part of the building, and a cabinetmaker rented part of the space. After the Glander brothers took over, they operated it as a partnership for about three years. In 1885, George sold his interest to Edward, who continued to run it as the Glander Brewery.

Born in Preble County, Edward Glander (1860–1912) continued to rent out part of the brewery to a cabinet shop. He also bought a saloon. He seemed to be moving away from the brewing business. An 1887 Sanborn insurance map marks the brewery site as the "old brewery." In 1890, he built icehouses and leased spring-fed ponds for a commercial ice operation. He rented much of the brewery to a tobacco company in 1900. By the time Darke County voted itself dry under the Rose law in 1908, as reported in the

November 1908 *The Western Brewer*, little of the brewery, if any, still involved beer. Glander rented the building to the Greenville Ice Cream Factory and the A. Friedberg & Bros. Tobacco Company.[76]

Union City

Union City didn't rise on the site of a frontier fort or spring up along a river. It owes its existence to railroads. In the late 1840s, the heads of two railroad companies—one in Indiana and one in Ohio—agreed to build separate lines that would butt together on the state line at a lonely spot in the wilderness, according to Andrew Olson in the *Indiana History Blog*. Joining two separately owned roads would create a transportation artery between Indianapolis and Bellefontaine, bisected by the state line. Union City itself shared the same split personality, a community divided by a political boundary.

The two railroads connected in 1853. Three more lines quickly followed. Because the railroad companies kept their trains on their own tracks, they had to stop in Union City to load and unload, creating local jobs. The remote town's population swelled; by 1880, more than 2,700 people lived on the Indiana side, with another 1,127 on the Ohio side, according to U.S. census records.

From the beginning, most Union City residents lived on the Indiana side. The town's first saloon opened there too. Some rowdy customers quickly earned it a place in local history. Authors W.H. McIntosh and E. Tucker both mentioned it in their books. McIntosh placed the saloon in Union City's first house: "In this structure a saloon was kept, whose baneful influence was attested by the simultaneous discharge of seventeen employees of the railroad shortly after its doors were thrown open." More saloons opened in the early 1850s, McIntosh added, "and so apparent were the ill effects of these institutions that a war against them was commenced and kept up until the evil traffic was abolished." Tucker's *History of Randolph County, Indiana* made a vague reference to "some pretty energetic measures" to stop the sale of alcohol. They closed the saloons on the Indiana side, but more than ever sprang up just across the state line. "There are now (1880) *thirteen* on the Ohio side," wrote McIntosh.

It would have been easy for saloons to get whiskey, either from local distilleries or by train. But beer didn't travel well before the era of refrigeration. It isn't clear when the first local brewery opened. The earliest

Left: The Old Hotel and Railroad Museum in Union City, Indiana. *Author's collection.*

Below: An 1865 map marked the location of Union City's brewery. *Map of Randolph County, Indiana.*

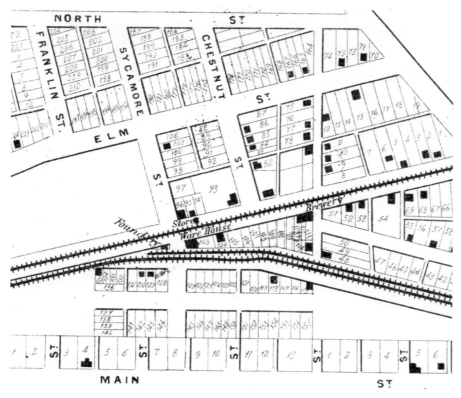

record found was C.S. Warner's 1865 *Map of Randolph County, Indiana*. It marks a brewery on the southwest corner where Division Street crosses the former Bellefontaine and Indianapolis Railroad, later a CSX line.[77]

The brewery's location seems odd at first glance. Beer's main ingredient is water, and the closest water in sight was Dismal Creek, a thousand feet to the south. As it turned out, an ample supply was underfoot. The same glaciers that shaped the landscape also left buried beds of sand, silt and clay, creating aquifers across the region. As of 1882, Tucker wrote, a single well met the needs of the town's four thousand inhabitants, serving up water "as though it were [from] an underground ocean."[78]

The brewery's proprietor was Louis Willaume (or Wuillaume, or Williams) (1835–1909), a French immigrant born in 1835. Some records indicate he came to Union City almost as soon as the trains did. A business directory in the 1875 Darke County atlas gave the year of his arrival as 1854. Tucker mentioned a "Lewis Gillaum had a shoe shop" in Union City in 1853.

Tucker might have been referring to "Willaume," a name that seemed to challenge writers and census takers. If one assumes Gillaum and Willaume were the same man, then he wasn't yet in the brewing business. But an 1860 census sheet found him working as a brewer in Piqua, thirty miles east of Union City. The census taker identified him as "Williams," but his first wife, the former Catharine Querstschy, gave her married name as "Wuillaume" in a will she wrote in 1861, shortly before she died at about age twenty-nine.

Louis remarried in 1862, still in Miami County. At some later date, he moved or returned to Union City with his second wife, Celestine Goubeaux, and their growing family.

Land records show Willaume bought half of Lots 112 and 113 in 1864, matching the brewery's location on the 1865 map. H.C. Chandler & Company's 1868 *Business Directory for Indiana* listed the Union City brewery under Willaume's name. The 1875 Darke County atlas describes him as "Louis Wuillaume, Proprietor of Restaurant and Brewery," at the southwest corner of Division Street and the railroad. He sold, it claimed, "beer and ale warranted to be made of nothing but pure Hops and Barley."

Wuillaume had the brewery for more than a decade. Published reports suggest it was the only commercial brewery in town. But a corner on the local beer market didn't mean life was easy. In 1871, he sued a government inspector for $5,000 in damages after the inspector, Willaume claimed, had him arrested for revenue violations of which he was later acquitted. In 1876, he advertised the brewery for sale at $4,000, or he would take a partner for $3,000. "Only one good brewery in the town," boasted his small ad on the

Louis Willaume (*in hat*) with daughter Anna Beardsley (*left*), granddaughter Elizabeth Beardsley Richie and great-grandson Kirby Richie. *Mrs. Ronald Richie Collection.*

front page of the April 13, 1876 *Cincinnati Daily Star.* "This is a good bargain on account of wanting to go back to France," it added.

It wasn't unusual for a brewer's children to take up the business, but none of Willaume's did. In 1878, Louis and Celestine were forced to sell the brewery property and two adjacent lots to pay off creditors. The 1880 census finds Louis still a brewer in Union City, living on Division Street close to the brewery, but the 1900 census identifies him as a widower and saloon owner.

Willaume's last move was to Bradford in Miami County, where he became the proprietor a business he dubbed "Louie's Place." His business card said it offered "fine wines, liquors, Beers and Cigars" with "no games" and "no bums." (The card gave his surname as "Willaume," apparently the spelling he preferred later in life.) He died in Bradford in 1909 and is buried as Louis Williams at Forest Hill Cemetery, Piqua. It isn't known if he ever got back to France.

Back in Union City, trains still thunder through town on the CSX line as of this writing, but they no longer stop. Next to the tracks, an old hotel houses a museum operated by the Preservation Society of Union City, Indiana. A few bars are in business, but no brewery has replaced Willaume's.[79]

New Madison

In the rainy, predawn darkness of April 30, 1865, a locomotive chugged slowly through New Madison, ten miles southwest of Greenville. Trains rumbling through this tiny community of fewer than five hundred weren't unusual, but hundreds of people stood solemnly in the rain to watch this one pass. In 2017, townsfolk dedicated a marker in front of the New Madison Public Library to memorialize the day Abraham Lincoln's funeral train carried the body of America's sixteenth president through town on its way to Springfield, Illinois, for burial.[80]

Railroads didn't create New Madison—its history dates from 1817—but the Lincoln Funeral Train's passage shows how the Indiana, Bloomington and Western Railroad must have loomed large in the small town's life in the mid-1800s. It brought transportation and commerce to a settlement far from the nearest canal or navigable river. "The village enjoys all the advantages of a railroad town," H.W. McIntosh wrote. It could also bring trouble.

John Lantry (born circa 1817), New Madison's earliest brewer of record, was an Irish immigrant who decided to switch from grocering to brewing sometime in the late 1850s. McIntosh wrote the brewery was built in 1858 and saw several additions until, by the 1870s, it was 144 feet long. The map of New Madison in the 1875 Darke County atlas shows a brewery extending halfway down the west side of Fayette Street from the corner at Main.

Lantry advertised in local papers. The Garst Museum in Greenville keeps a small ad, dated 1866, clipped from an unidentified newspaper. It describes Lantry as a "Manufacturer of Ale & Beer," adding, "All work guaranteed to be of the latest style and to give entire satisfaction."

Lantry's brewery became known for its pungent aroma. "It has been said by some of the old timers that the scent of the beer brewed there was so strong that it could lift a man's hat right off his head if he didn't hold it," Glen Hindsley wrote in *Yester Years of New Madison Ohio*.

Lantry's brewery figured in a fatal altercation among some railroad workers. Along with commerce, the railroad brought workers "who visited the town in squads and spent their money freely for whisky, beer, &c., seldom, if at all, returning sober," according to an undated news clipping from a local scrapbook collection. One evening, a twenty-five-year-old man named William Noggle had been drinking with some railroaders when they broke into a fight outside the brewery. Noggle, known to be a "rough customer," according to the article, found a rock or a brick and heaved it, hitting a man named David Dudgeon above the left eye. Noggle fled, and

Houses on Fayette Street in New Madison occupy the site of John Lantry's brewery. *Author's collection.*

Dudgeon died several days later. Noggle was still eluding authorities as the article was written.

The brewery had a short run, evidently because Lantry was increasingly suffering from a rheumatic disorder—"rheumatism," the 1880 census put it—a condition affecting joints and connective tissues that can be painful and disabling. "Since 1875, the brewery has been idle. Mr. Lantry is disabled so that he seldom leaves the premises," McIntosh wrote. Lantry was about sixty-three at the time. No record could be found of Lantry's death or the fate of his brewery. Houses eventually replaced it.[81]

CHAPTER 8

SPRINGFIELD

THE BRITISH INVASION

A t West Main and Fisher Streets in downtown Springfield, a statue of a pioneer woman stands as of this writing, her face stoic under a bonnet's brim, her left arm cradling a baby and her right hand gripping a rifle, striding resolutely forward with a boy clinging to her long skirts.

This is the Madonna of the Trail, one of a dozen such statues commissioned by the Daughters of the American Revolution in the early twentieth century to commemorate the building of the National Road. Although it eventually spanned the continent, the road began as America's first federally funded interstate highway, conceived by George Washington and authorized by Thomas Jefferson to connect the young nation's eastern coast to the Ohio frontier. Extended across the state in the 1830s, it passed north of Dayton but went right through the heart of Springfield.

Springfield lies twenty miles northeast of Dayton in Clark County. In its earliest years, it lacked direct access to the transportation arteries of the Great Miami River and the Miami and Erie Canal. The highway provided an alternate route to eastern markets. Decades before the National Road, Springfield's first settlers came from the east. Griffith Foos led the first group of settlers from Franklinton (later Columbus) in 1801, according to William M. Rockel's *20th Century History of Springfield and Clark County*.[82]

Madonna of the Trail
monument in downtown
Springfield. *Author's collection.*

PIONEER BREWERS

The cabin Foos built that year doubled as the town's first tavern. In 1803, Archibald Lowry built a much larger, two-story tavern of hewn logs. Whether those taverns served beer isn't known, but Benjamin F. Prince wrote in *A Standard History of Springfield and Clark County, Ohio* that in 1804, "Foos and Lowry had taverns, and there was a brewery."

Beer brewing grew with the community. By 1832, Rockel wrote, the village of 1,250 people included "4 churches, one paper mill, one grist mill and one carding and fulling [or felting] mill, one brewery and one distillery."

No names surfaced for those pioneer breweries or their owners. The earliest of record were the Springfield Brewery and the City Brewery.

An 1852 advertisement for Joseph James W. Brain's brewery, later the Springfield Brewery. *Directory of the City of Springfield, 1852.*

The Springfield Brewery stood at the northeast corner of Columbia and Spring Streets, near the center of town. The City Brewery was built on the side of a hill at the southwest corner of Penn and Section Streets, a block south and two blocks east of the Springfield Brewery. It isn't clear when the breweries acquired their names, as most records identify them by their owners. But both establishments remained in business under a succession of owners throughout the nineteenth century and into the twentieth. The Springfield Brewery started in 1840, followed by the City Brewery in 1849, according to Beers's *The History of Clark County, Ohio.*[83]

The earliest brewer identified with either site was Joseph James W. Brain (1816–1855), an English immigrant. Land records show he owned the Springfield Brewery site as early as 1845, when he bought the property in a court-ordered auction. He was brewing about eight hundred barrels of beer per year in 1850, according to that year's census of industrial production. He advertised as "J.W. Brain, Brewer and Maltster," in Stephenson & Company's 1852 *Directory of the City of Springfield.*

Vorce and Blee

Brain died in 1855. In 1858, his son, George, acting as executor of his father's estate, sold the brewery to Silas A. Vorce and Charles G. Everett for $6,250. Everett, a tanner from Prussia, sold his share to Vorce the next year for $5,800. Born in New York, Silas A. Vorce (circa 1818–1860) had lived for a time in Cleveland, where he married Martha W. Gardner (1819–1900), a Cleveland native. Silas had worked as postmaster in Wickliffe and Willoughby, near Cleveland, before moving to Springfield sometime in the 1850s. Both were of undetermined descent, although Charles Marvin Vorce, in *A Genealogical and Historical Record of the Vorce Family in America*, placed Silas's ancestors in France.

Silas had the brewery a short time. He died in December 1860 at about age forty-two, leaving the brewery—and three children, two not yet fully grown—in the hands of his forty-one-year-old widow.

Following her husband's wish that she "carry on my business of brewing," as Silas wrote in his will, Martha worked to collect outstanding debts and pay off her own, while keeping the brewery up and running. "I am now prepared to pay cash prices for Barley and Rye. I keep constantly on hand and for sale, a pure article of ale and beer, also Barley and Rye Malt and Hops," she announced in the October 7, 1861 issue of the *Springfield Republic*. She ran the brewery until 1866 as "M.W. Vorce," making her the Miami Valley's earliest woman brewery proprietor of record.

In the space of a few decades, Springfield had grown from a pioneer village to a bustling midwestern town. Spurring Springfield's growth was its rise as a manufacturing center for farm machinery. By 1860, U.S. census figures show, its population topped seven thousand and nearly doubled during that decade. Railroads connected Springfield with major cities.

It's uncertain how often, if ever, Martha's eldest daughter, Achsa, hopped on a train to visit relatives in Cleveland, but somehow she crossed paths with William H. Blee (1842–1917). Census records and city directories show he was the son of a successful Irish grocer who lived in Martha's hometown neighborhood. Two passport applications describe him as standing six feet, two inches, with sandy hair, blue eyes, a high forehead and a straight nose.

Blee worked as a railroad conductor sometime in the early 1860s. It's likely no coincidence his eldest brother, Robert—a future mayor of Cleveland—was working his way up to superintendent of the "CC&CRR," the Cleveland, Columbus and Cincinnati Railroad. William and other brothers also found jobs there. William and Achsa could have met in Cleveland or Springfield any

SPRINGFIELD

Brewery and Malt House,

SPRINGFIELD, OHIO.

S. A. VORCE,

MANUFACTURER OF

RYE AND BARLEY MALT

BEER & ALE,

AND DEALER IN

HOPS,

WHOLESALE & RETAIL.

Orders by mail accompanied with the CASH promptly attended to.

Casks should be corked as soon as emptied to avoid must,

Iron Hooped Casks,	$2 00
Half Barrels	1 50
Kegs,	1 00

Prices of Casks always charged with their contents, and on their return in good order, the same amount refunded.

Left: An 1859 advertisement by S.A. Vorce for the Springfield Brewery and Malt House. *Directory of the City of Springfield, 1859.*

Below: After her husband's death, Martha W. Vorce took over the Springfield Brewery. *Springfield Republic.*

Springfield Brewery!

PARTIES having claims against the Estate of S. A. Vorce, deceased, will please present the same at the Springfield Brewery for payment, and it is also desirable that all those indebted to the Estate call at the above mentioned place and settle immediately.

I am now prepared to pay cash prices for Barley and Rye.

I keep constantly on hand, and for sale, a pure article of ALE and BEER, also Barley and Rye Malt and Hops.   M. W. VORCE, Executrix.

oct2 4w

number of ways, but one can imagine it happening on a train on CC&CRR's Springfield branch, their eyes meeting as William worked his way down the aisle of the swaying car, punching tickets. However it happened, Clark County marriage records show they were wed in October 1864.

Two years later, Martha Vorce gave up the brewery for unknown reasons. Land records show she sold it for $15,000 to Charles H. Evans, John H. Littler and Silas F. Edgar, doing business as Charles H. Evans & Company. Records reveal little about them, but Springfield had attorneys named Evans and Littler in the 1870s and a physician named Silas F. Edgar. Cleveland city directories and Cuyahoga County tax records indicate Martha moved back to Cleveland, where her name resurfaced in her old neighborhood on Bolivar and Prospect Avenue through 1869. William Blee appeared in the same records as a nearby resident, presumably with Achsa.

Clark County land records show Martha Vorce bought back the brewery in a public auction in 1869. It followed a lawsuit she filed against Evans & Company that forced them to turn the brewery over to a receiver. Martha paid $12,000 for the real estate and another $1,506 for personal property. Altogether, she paid not quite what she had sold it for two years earlier. The 1870 census also found Blee back in Springfield, where he joined her in the brewing business. The Springfield Brewery began to operate as Vorce and Blee, a label that would stick for nearly two decades.

While Martha owned the brewery and their business named her first, public records show no acknowledgement of her as a business leader. Her son-in-law, meanwhile, became president of the Owen Machine Tool Company, vice-president of the Springfield Savings Bank and a member of the Springfield City Council. It was at a time when American women lacked many rights, including the right to vote.

Martha eventually married Cornelius Baker. William and Achsa became part owners of the brewery, along with Achsa's sisters Ella and Clara. The Springfield Brewery continued to run as Vorce and Blee until 1890, when international investors transformed the city's brewing industry.[84]

CITY BREWERY

While Joseph Brain was tending his brew kettle at Columbia and Spring Streets, Jacob Huben and Joseph Leibold started making beer at Penn and Section. Land records indicate they started it in 1849.

Huben (1819–1899) was an immigrant from the Lorraine area of northeastern France. Leibold (1823–1877) came from the province of Hohenzollern, later in the state of Baden-Württemberg in southern Germany. They brewed together until 1862, when Huben and his wife, Christina, sold their half interest to Leibold for $10,000. Two years later, Leibold sold the brewery to Ethan A. Williams and William B. Baker. In 1866, Baker and his wife, Huldah, apparently as sole owners, sold the brewery for $24,000 to a pair of Baden emigrants, Casper Engert (1818–1888) and Stephen Dinkel (1836–1884). The terms included Baker's agreement not to engage in brewing within five miles of the brewery for five years.

Engert and Dinkel brewed "ale and lager beer" in the 1870s, according to Swartz and Tedrowe's *Springfield Directory, 1873–1874*. They sold 6,609 barrels in 1878 and 7,160 in 1879, according to Salem's *Beer, Its History and Its Economic Value as a National Beverage*.

Some of their numerous children worked in the brewery at various times. John Dinkel, Stephen's eldest child, appears as a brewer in A. Bailey's 1870 *Dayton Directory* (which included Springfield), when he would have been about thirteen, as well as in the 1880 census at age twenty-three. His younger

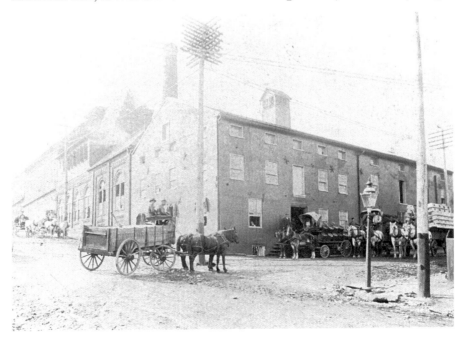

An undated photo of the old City Brewery, renamed Springfield Breweries Ltd. *Clark County Historical Society.*

brother Joseph was working as a cellarman at about age twelve, according to the 1875 *Williams' Springfield Directory*. Neither one succeeded Engert; he sold his interest to Dinkel in 1882 for $35,000. The sale included land for an ice pond on about twelve acres north of the brewery, roughly bounded by what were then Nelson Avenue on the south; the Cincinnati, Sandusky and Cleveland Railroad on the east; and Buck Creek on the north and west. The terms included the right to flow water from the creek onto the tract.

Dinkel owned the brewery barely two years before he died. His heirs sold it in 1884 to the Schneider brothers—Charles, August and Joseph. The deed transfer records identify their wives as Katie, Helene and Josephine, respectively, but little more about the Schneiders could be found. But their run as independent brewers was brief.[85]

THE BRITISH INVASION

In the late 1800s, British investors were buying a wide range of U.S. companies. Among food- and drink-related producers, the British were particularly enamored of American breweries, according to economic and business historian Mira Wilkins. "Investments in U.S. beer making were part of a merry round of promotions, with the British intoxicated by the prospect of profits," she wrote in *The History of Foreign Investment in the United States to 1914*. Between 1888 and 1891, twenty-four British investment groups, or syndicates, bought about eighty American breweries from coast to coast. It wasn't unusual for a syndicate to merge two or more breweries in a city and consolidate their operations, just as American investors were forming combines.

Springfield's turn came in 1890. In March that year, *The Economist* announced the formation of the Springfield Breweries Ltd. Its purpose was to buy both of Springfield's breweries and operate them under one management, it reported.

Land records show the Schneider brothers fetched $120,000 for their brewery, while Vorce and Blee got only $50,000. Why there was such a difference in prices is unclear. No figures turned up for their individual assets, revenues or profits at that time.

The new, London-based directors kept local managers in place. *Williams' Springfield City Directory for 1890–1891* listed William H. Blee, Joseph Schneider and William R. Burnett—Springfield's mayor at the time—as directors, with

Another view of the old City Brewery. *Clark County Historical Society.*

Charles Schneider as manager and L. Phillips as secretary-treasurer. Blee remained a director until his death in 1917.

The City Brewery appeared in the 1890 directory as Schneider Brothers, "brewers and bottlers of celebrated Vienna Beer." The Springfield Brewery brewed and bottled "ale, porter and lager beer." Both plants continued to operate. They sold a variety of beers, but they became known for Red Head beer, made at the original Springfield Brewery plant, and Blue Head beer, made at the former City Brewery—so much so the individual plants were sometimes called the "Red Head Brewery" or the "Blue Head Brewery." The 1898 *Brewer's Guide* put the company's total annual sales between thirty-five and forty thousand barrels.[86]

HOME CITY BREWING

Springfield Breweries Ltd. enjoyed a monopoly for a few years, at least locally. This ended in 1905 when a group of local saloon owners incorporated the Home City Brewing Company. It was a complete startup: capitalized at $100,000, the company built a new brewery at 500 West Main Street, later renumbered 1100 West Main, on the northwest corner of West Main and South Bell Avenue. The brewery included its own bottling and ice plants, and a railroad siding gave it direct access to the Big Four railroad line skirting the brewery. It was to have a capacity of twenty-five to thirty-five thousand barrels. City directories began listing it in 1907.[87]

A vestige of the old City Brewery survived in 2018 at Penn and Section Streets. *Author's collection.*

The name "Home City Brewing" reflected Springfield's growing pride in becoming a place for institutional homes. Several national fraternal organizations built them around the turn of the century to care for members and their families. First was the Ohio Masonic Home, according to Rockel; it was a large campus of residential and care facilities built along the National Road west of Springfield. City directories show only two other Springfield businesses used "Home City" in their names when the Home City Brewing Company was formed in 1905; by 1910, five did so. The nickname faded in time, although the Masons continue to operate and modernize their home as of this writing.

The president of Home City Brewing was John L. Coleman (1860–1935), an Irish immigrant who came to America in 1879. The brewery wasn't Coleman's only concern: *Williams' Springfield City Directory for 1907* describes him as a dealer in coal, coke and cement; proprietor of the "Celebrated Half-Way Home Saloon"; and president of the brewing company. He remained president until 1912 and then stepped down to secretary; he left the board in 1914, possibly to focus on his saloon and coal businesses.

Springfield Breweries and Home City Brewing continued to satisfy local palates even as breweries in other Ohio counties shut down in the wake of local option elections—even, quietly, into the Prohibition era.[88]

CHAPTER 9

PROHIBITION AND AFTERMATH

It had been out there for ages, like a distant asteroid on a collision course with Earth. Everyone saw it coming, and many looked for ways to deflect it, delay it or lessen its impact. But its arrival was as sudden and devastating as the space rock that wiped out the dinosaurs. It was Prohibition, and it was the beer industry's killer asteroid.

Decades of protests and debates led Congress on December 3, 1917, to pass a joint resolution approving language for a Constitutional amendment. Starting one year after ratification, it would prohibit "the manufacture, sale, or transportation of intoxicating liquors" within the United States and all territories under U.S. jurisdiction. It required ratification by at least thirty-six of the nation's forty-eight states. (Alaska and Hawaii were still territories.)

Congress gave the states seven years to do it. It took thirteen months. Nebraska, Missouri and Wyoming approved it on January 16, 1919, completing ratification.

Ohio's legislature ratified the amendment on January 7 that year, but it wasn't a popular move. Ohio voters overturned it in a referendum. Prohibition supporters challenged the referendum. The Ohio Supreme Court ruled against them, but on June 1, 1920, the U.S. Supreme Court upheld Ohio's ratification. Underscoring how divisive the issue was in Ohio, voters narrowly approved a statewide prohibition amendment in November 1918. It was effective May 27, 1919, ahead of national Prohibition.[89]

This 1874 illustration by C.S. Reinhart shows women in a saloon, protesting the sale of alcoholic beverages. *From* Harper's Weekly.

Deep Roots

In truth, America's prohibition movement was almost as old as the industry it opposed. It evolved from what early proponents called temperance. An early effort to create a national movement was the American Temperance Society (later Union), formed in Boston in 1826, according to Ernest H. Cherrington's *Evolution of Prohibition in the United States of America*. Chapters sprang up around the country, including in Ohio. Other organizations also arose, among them the Sons of Temperance and a splinter group, the Order of Templars of Honor and Temperance. It opened its grand temple in New York City in 1846 and opened other temples elsewhere, including a grand temple in Cincinnati and satellite temples around Ohio.

The monthly journal *Templar's Magazine*, published by Cincinnati's grand temple, offered a glimpse of the Miami Valley as it appeared in the eyes of a fervent temperance reformer. Editor J. Wadsworth's November 1850 column describes a trip up the valley to visit other temples. Following a pleasant trip by undescribed means from Cincinnati to Lebanon,

Wadsworth survived a wild ride to Dayton "by stage, in an old rickety coach belonging to the Voorhees & Co.'s line." The coach had a faulty brake, Wadsworth wrote, "and the way we traveled down hill was a caution of 'Jehu,'" a reference to an Israeli king noted in the Bible for his furious method of driving chariots.

From Dayton, Troy was a languid, seven-hour ride up the Miami & Erie Canal on a horse-drawn packet boat. Packets were the canal's passenger boats, and at least some had small bars stocked with liquor. Wadsworth noted

> *an unusual number of calls at the Bar of the boat. The individual who officiated as Captain from Cincinnati to Dayton was so much under the influence of alcohol that he gave up his post to another at Dayton, and turned in and was not visible again until we left the boat.... When will these nuisances called bars on canal and steamboats be abated so that sober people can travel with comfort and safety?*[290]

WOMAN'S TEMPERANCE CRUSADE

What became known as the Woman's Temperance Crusade took off in Ohio at the end of 1873 with a lecture in Hillsboro by "Dr." Dio Lewis, then of Boston. Lewis was a self-styled physician of homeopathy whose teachings included exercise and temperance. In lectures exhorting women to organize against liquor sellers, Lewis shared his own moving story, as related in Reverend W.C. Steel's *Woman's Temperance Movement*, about a father who "had forgotten everything but drink" and an abused mother who sustained herself with prayer.

On December 23, Lewis's lecture in the town's Music Hall lit a fire under women. Located about fifty miles southeast of Dayton, Hillsboro was the seat of rural Highland County, with two women's colleges and its share of saloons. He found an educated and attentive audience, "and when Dr Lewis asked if they were willing to undertake the task, scores of women rose to their feet," Wittenmyer wrote in *History of the Woman's Temperance Crusade*.

They organized the next day and launched a campaign against local saloons and druggists who sold liquor. They succeeded in closing Hillsboro's saloons and energized women in other towns to follow their example. Similar crusades took place around Ohio and across the nation. They were effective in some villages, less so in cities. Because Ohio women were at the forefront

Because Ohio women were at the forefront of the 1874 temperance crusade, it also became known as the "Ohio Whisky War" and the "Women's Whiskey War." *From* Frank Leslie's Illustrated Newspaper.

of the 1874 temperance crusade, pundits also dubbed it the "Ohio Whisky War" and the "Women's Whiskey War."

In Dayton, where Wittenmyer calculated there was a bar for every twelve families, saloons besieged by praying women offered free beer and whiskey. She quoted a *Cincinnati Gazette* correspondent who observed, "The result was, more drunken men on the streets than had been seen since the 4th of July." The vigils continued, but in April, brewery-friendly candidates prevailed in a city council election—including Lawrence Butz Jr. A German immigrant and grocer, Butz had been Henry Ferneding's partner in the City Brewery for a few years in the early 1860s. Wittenmyer labeled him "the whiskey candidate."

Piqua was daunting, with "a large German population; heavy wholesale liquor houses, and wealthy men who rented their property to liquor-dealers," Wittenmyer wrote, admitting the crusade there saw mixed success: "Many saloon keepers gave up the business, others became violent and insulting....In one saloon a mock prayer meeting was held and the Lord's Supper celebrated with beer and crackers by saloon keepers and their drunken customers."[91]

MOTHER STEWART

The crusade in Springfield had its own history. Long before Dio Lewis showed up, Eliza Daniel Stewart was working as a community organizer. Her activities drew press attention, and a *Dayton Journal* editorial declared that she was "on a temperance crusade against liquor-selling." In *Memories of the Crusade*, Stewart credited the undated editorial with naming the crusade.

Portrait of Eliza Daniel "Mother" Stewart. *Clark County Historical Society.*

Born Eliza Daniel (1816–1908) in Piketon in 1816, Stewart lost both of her parents before she was twelve, but through work in her church, she managed to build a career as a teacher. Her first husband died soon after her marriage, but with her second she became a charter member of the local Good Templar Lodge, according to a biographical sketch.

She gathered supplies for soldiers during the Civil War and visited them in hospitals, where she gained the nickname "Mother." After the war, the sight of soldiers succumbing to alcohol stirred her to oppose liquor sales. "Mother Stewart" became widely known after moving to Springfield, where a lecture she delivered on January 22, 1872, marked her debut as a crusader.

In *A Woman of the Century*, Frances Willard and Mary Livermore detailed Stewart's leading role as the movement gathered steam. On December 2, 1873, Stewart organized a Woman's League in Osborne (now Fairborn), forerunner of the WCTU. She was prominent in Springfield and elsewhere during the crusade, and she became an early leader in the WCTU. In 1876, she spent five months in Great Britain, lecturing and helping to organize the British Women's Temperance Association.[92]

Stewart was one of many Ohio prohibitionists who had a national impact. The crusade led to the formation of the WCTU in Cleveland in November 1874. The Anti Saloon League formed in Oberlin, Ohio, in May 1893 as the Ohio Anti-Saloon League. A similar organization formed in Washington, D.C., the same year, and the two organizations merged to form what would become the National Anti-Saloon League, a powerful force in the Prohibition movement.

CARRIE NATION

Another crusader with an Ohio connection was its most notorious: the six-foot, 175-pound, hatchet-wielding, saloon-crashing Carrie A. Nation.

Born on a Kentucky farm, Carrie Amelia Moore (1846–1911) lived in several places as a child before her family settled in Cass County, Missouri, near Kansas City. She experienced a religious conversion at the age of ten and was deeply religious for the rest of her life.

In the fall of 1865, a young medical doctor and Civil War veteran approached the Moores seeking board. He was Charles Gloyd (1840–1869), the son of Harry Gloyd (1799–1868). Biographical sources and census records show Harry Gloyd was a Vermont native who moved to Shelby County. He served as justice of the peace and kept a tavern in the tiny hamlet of Newport, about eleven miles west of Sidney.

Charles Gloyd was a studious young man who spoke several languages. Carrie "stood in awe of him," she wrote in her autobiography. They fell in love and married on November 21, 1867. "My father and mother warned me that the doctor was addicted to drink but I had no idea of the curse of rum," she wrote. She soon learned he was a severe alcoholic who drank in the Masonic Lodge while his medical practice faded.

Gloyd's mother blamed army life for introducing her son to drink. Nation blamed the Masons and secret societies in general for encouraging drinking, and she blamed "this liquor evil" itself as a malevolent entity. She left him and returned to her parents, where she gave birth to their daughter. Gloyd begged her to come back. "He said: 'Pet, if you leave me, I will be a dead man in six months,'" she wrote. He was right. She learned of his death in a telegram.[93]

She worked as a teacher until she married David Nation, a journalist, lawyer and preacher. They moved to Texas for a time and then to Medicine Lodge, Kansas. She organized a local WCTU chapter and led a crusade that closed the saloons in Medicine Lodge.

Nation stormed into the national spotlight in 1900, when she believed God told her to close the bars in Kiowa, Kansas. There she attacked the saloons with bricks. In 1901, she attacked bars in Topeka with what would become her trademark, a small hatchet. Newspapers made her a celebrity, but her marriage fell apart and she was divorced by the end of 1901. To make ends meet, she went on the speaking circuit and sold pewter hatchets as souvenirs. In 1903, she changed her name from Carrie to "Carry," saying her name meant "Carry A. Nation for Prohibition."

Carrie A. Nation. *Library of Congress.*

Nation came to Dayton on September 24, 1904—not to smash saloons but to lecture on their evils and promote the Prohibition Party's candidate for president against the Republican incumbent, Theodore Roosevelt. She returned on October 20 and made several appearances over the next few days.

During her second visit, a local man identified as Walter Ross donned a "Mother Hubbard" dress and a sun bonnet and "with a wooden ax, paraded along Third Street until arrested," according to the *Dayton Daily News*. The paper speculated "a saloon keeper, fond of a jest," put him up to it "and that he was told to pretend that he was the great saloon smasher."[94]

DRY OHIO

Around the country, Prohibition made inroads at the state and local levels years before Congress opened the door to Constitutional change. Ohio saw a series of laws aimed at allowing voters to hold local option elections at the precinct, township, city or county level. By 1908, five of Ohio's eighty-eight counties had gone dry in local option elections. That year, the new Rose law triggered sixty-eight countywide elections that took fifty-seven counties dry.

Montgomery stayed wet, but the Dayton Breweries Company wasn't complacent. In December 1907, Adam Schantz filled two pages of the *Dayton Daily News* with a letter detailing how the company had been buying up and shutting down troublesome saloons, eliminating any need for local option elections. In June 1908, Dayton Breweries published a special section in the *Dayton Journal* with pictures of its breweries and long features about the "industrial importance of the brewer's art." It calculated Dayton's breweries, saloons and other "allied trades"—from barrel makers to National Cash Register (later NCR)—provided five thousand jobs supporting as many families, or, as it estimated, twenty-five thousand individuals, a fifth of the city's population.

The company also repeated the industry's mantra that beer was good for you. "The high percentage of malt used in its production makes it one of the best tonics that human ingenuity has produced," it asserted. And it argued past attempts at prohibition by other states only resulted in "moral deception, political corruption and the evasion of law."

As president of the Ohio Brewers' Association, Schantz organized a "Vigilance Bureau" to monitor saloons. Under his direction, "a corps of secret service men working in different parts of the state have done much good in the eradication of disreputable places," it reported.[95]

But the Prohibition movement gained ground. In 1917 and 1918, the Ohio Anti-Saloon League formed the Ohio Dry Federation to unite all the state's temperance and prohibition groups. The federation spent nearly $1 million on campaigns for statewide prohibition. It also produced illustrations and cartoons for use by the press, much of it playing to patriotic and anti-German sentiment in conjunction with America's entry into World War I. The payoff came in November 1919, with passage of Ohio's own prohibition amendment.[96]

The Great Contraction

The relentless march toward Prohibition put Dayton Breweries under increasing pressure. Less than two years after Schantz had confidently predicted business growth would keep all the combined breweries in production, Dayton Breweries turned the old City Brewery on South Brown Street—formerly Jacob Stickle's brewery—into a bottling plant, the *Dayton Daily News* reported.

Acquisition of Nick Thomas's Hydraulic Brewery in September 1906 allowed even more consolidation. Thomas had just modernized his plant and boosted capacity to 150,000 barrels. Dayton Breweries decided to end brewing at Schantz's aging Riverside Brewery in 1907, although it continued to produce its popular Lily Water. It changed the name of Nick Thomas's brewery to Schantz Thomas.

World War I prompted several nations to prohibit brewing and distilling in order to conserve food and fuel. U.S. prohibitionists used the same reasons to press for restrictions on brewers' use of grains and coal. Empowered by Congress, W.J. Rorabaugh wrote in *Prohibition: A Concise History*, President Wilson, in December 1917, ordered breweries to reduce grain usage by 30 percent; in July 1918, he halved their coal allotments.[97]

The impact of the coal restriction was almost immediate, according to the *Dayton Daily News*. The next month, Dayton Breweries shuttered the Dayton View (or Schwind) brewery and the Schantz and Schwind (or Gem City) brewery. It gave its massive Riverside brewery to the new Miami Conservancy District, which eventually tore it town. (The old brewery stood in the way of the district's riverbank realignment project, part of a sweeping flood control program aimed at preventing a recurrence of the Great Dayton Flood that had ravaged the Miami Valley in 1913.)

The grand consolidation was becoming the great contraction. The local press reported one sale or shutdown after another. In 1919, the Lake Coal and Ice Company bought the Wehner plant in Edgemont and used it to make ice for several years until the plant was demolished. The Lowe Brothers Paint Company bought the former Sachs-Pruden plant on Wyandotte. Cleveland ice cream maker Telling-Belle Vernon bought the Schantz and Schwind plant. By 1920, Dayton Breweries had moved its offices into the former N. Thomas plant at First and Beckel, where it then produced near beer and other soft drinks.

In 1919, the G.H. Shartzer Company took over the old Schwind brewery and advertised a huge liquidation sale. The inventory included lumber, furniture, engines, pipes, pumps, tanks, tubs and the brewery's 140-barrel brew kettle—but no beer. Finally, Shartzer began dismantling the hollowed-out plant. The fall of its 150-foot-tall brick smokestack a year later marked the end of an era. Dayton Breweries defaulted on bond payments in 1921, and a court-appointed receiver auctioned its remaining assets in November.[98]

THE LAST BREWERIES

In Springfield, Home City Brewing's modern plant kept brewing right up until Prohibition—and then some. Times were tough. The brewery fell into receivership in 1920, and a new company began operating the plant in 1921 as the Home City Beverage Company. Like other, similarly renamed breweries, it produced non-alcoholic beverages. But on the night of February 2, 1925, U.S. marshals raided the brewery, according to a later newspaper report. They found the plant had been producing the real stuff on weekends. Hooking a hose to the brewery's tanks, the agents drained 9,600 gallons of beer into a storm sewer. The brewery was padlocked, and company officers and employees went to jail, along with some Cincinnati-area café owners who had been buying the beer. Home City resumed business as an ice and cold storage locker until its demolition in 1974.

No such exciting times were reported for Springfield Breweries. With Prohibition, it began producing Red Head near beer, sodas and ice. Martin H. Huonker and Charles A. Hartmann kept it in business through Prohibition, afterward focusing on beer distribution and ice making. In 1938, Springfield Coal and Ice co-located with its offices at 118 North Spring Street, and after 1956, only the coal business appeared in city directories.[99]

Back in Dayton, the old Nick Thomas–Dayton Breweries plant at First and Beckel saw new life as the Miami Valley Brewing Company, appearing in city directories in 1924. It sold non-alcoholic products until the repeal of Prohibition allowed the company to resume brewing beer. City directories found it producing a wide variety of beers under the Nick Thomas, London Bobby and Van Beck brands until the middle of the century.

The Olt Brewing Company—later Olt Brothers Brewing—had Dayton's newest beer plant. Without the overhead costs of old facilities and excess capacity, it was in better shape to switch to the alcohol-free marketplace of Prohibition. It sold near beer and added Polar Distilled Water, a product it kept after Prohibition.

A Home City Brewing coaster is a reminder of pre-Prohibition times in Springfield. *Clark County Historical Society.*

Olt brought back its popular Superba beer sometime after the end of Prohibition. An ad in the 1941 *Williams' Buyers Guide of*

A stable of the Olt Brothers brewery still stands at the southwest corner of Second and McGee in Dayton. *Author's collection.*

the City of Dayton promoted its "New Superba Beer" as "Full Enjoyment—Never a Headache!" Olt ended beer production in 1942, but its flagship beer is memorialized in east Dayton, where Superba Court marks the brewery site. A brick building that once housed a stable still stands as of this writing.

Theodore D. Hollenkamp met Prohibition by reorganizing his Dayton company as Hollenkamp Products Company and announcing plans to make near beer, soft drinks and ices. The company struggled through Prohibition with cereal beverages and as a distributor of Whistle orange soda, resuming beer production after 1933. The family sold it around 1940, and it operated under several names into the 1960s—first as the Airline Brewing Company and later as Ol-Fashion Brewing Company and Dayton Brewing Corporation, which produced the Kitty Hawk line of cream ale and lager.

By the close of the decade, the local beer brands no longer appeared in publications. The story of brewing in the Dayton region was over. It would take a new generation of beer-loving entrepreneurs to start a new one. But they would do it by drawing on all that had come before.[100]

CHAPTER 10

REBIRTH

In a large courtyard in the heart of downtown Springfield, the stern visages of Mother Stewart and Carrie Nation glare down from brick walls on a scene that would have made their blood boil: people drinking beer. And, consciously or not, toasting their memories.

The courtyard is the beer garden of Mother Stewart's Brewing Company. It's named after Eliza Daniel "Mother" Stewart, Springfield's hometown temperance crusader, who rests a mile away in Ferncliff Cemetery. Adjacent to the courtyard is the nineteenth-century brick warehouse where the brewery and taproom opened in 2016, bringing Springfield's once-vibrant brewing industry back from the dead—in the warehouse of a casket factory.

The warehouse is one in a cluster of downtown industrial buildings that once were home to the Springfield Metallic Casket Company. Between Mother Stewart and a casket factory, it's hard to imagine a more ironic name and place for the resurrection of local brewing. But irony wasn't why brothers Kevin and John Loftis decided to start a brewery.

Kevin Loftis grew up in Springfield, but he was attending the University of Vermont in Burlington in the 1990s when he first flirted with a brewing career. He took a part-time job with Otter Creek, then a startup brewery in Middlebury. The part-time job became a full-time passion, and Loftis took an educational detour to study brewing at the Siebel Institute in Chicago. But he left the brewery, and brewing, in 1998 to work for a while in adventure travel before returning to Springfield and joining his father in the real estate business. Loftis toyed with the

Kevin Loftis, co-owner of Mother Stewart's Brewing in Springfield. *Author's collection.*

idea of opening a microbrewery in 2005, but "Springfield didn't seem ready," he said in a 2017 interview.

The situation began to change in 2011, when the Ohio legislature passed a bill allowing breweries to sell beer on their premises without having to pay for a secondary permit. The state took an even bigger step in 2013 when it created a new liquor permit for small brewers. The new permit dropped the licensing cost from nearly $8,000 to $1,000. Across the state, the new rules were a game changer for struggling microbrewers and many more, like Loftis, who had been watching from the sidelines.

The change came at the right time for Kevin and his brother, John, who worked in construction. "I was burned out on real estate. My brother was burned out on construction," Kevin said. They began to talk about starting a brewery, and the old casket warehouse came to mind. As a real estate professional, "I had tried to develop it for eight years," Kevin said. It had just what they needed: plenty of space for a large production system, taproom and storage and the rustic charm of old brick walls and wood beams. They applied their skills to repurpose the building, and Kevin resurrected his knowledge of brewing and breweries.

But why name it for someone who had been known internationally for her relentless crusade against alcohol? Kevin said they researched local history for names. They wanted something that would reflect their community but would also appeal to a broader market. "I kept coming back to Mother Stewart's," he said. "It's local, and beyond that, it's an unforgettable name." Also, the name was free of trademark restrictions.

A few people in town "didn't think it was very funny" to name a brewery after a once-famous prohibitionist, Loftis admitted, but he argued it brought an important historical figure back from obscurity: "People forty and under had no idea who she was. Now everybody knows."[101]

False Starts and Sudden Success

The Loftis brothers had reason for caution under Ohio's old brewery rules. The Miami Valley saw several false starts. In Xenia, the Miami Trail Brewing Company opened in the 1990s, only to fold in the early 2000s. Several microbrewers launched businesses in Montgomery County in the 1990s. The longest-lived effort was Thirsty Dog Grille and Brewery in Centerville, which closed in 2005.

Even beer-loving Minster was the scene of a microbrewery failure. Two local brewers revived the Wooden Shoe brand in 2005, selling contract-brewed beer until they began brewing their own in 2010. The brewery closed in 2012 when the partnership dissolved, according to a news report.

Ohio found itself trailing what had become a national craft beer trend. But there was enough interest to prompt the formation of the Ohio Craft Brewers Association in Columbus in 2008. With the first big reform in 2011, craft brewing surged statewide. Between 2011 and 2018, the number of breweries in Ohio swelled from just over 40 to 299, with 65 more planned, according to the association. As of this writing, the association ranks Ohio fourth in craft beer production among U.S. states, with a statewide economic impact of $2.67 billion.[102]

The ability to include a taproom (also called a tasting room) with a brewery made a big difference, northern Ohio brewers told the *Toledo Blade* in 2014. Besides providing a sales outlet, it allowed brewers to hear directly from their customers. Down in the Miami Valley, the *Dayton City Paper* in August 2011 anticipated the Gem City's first new brewery in half a century as the Toxic Brew Company prepared for a 2012 opening in an old Oregon District pawn shop. "Will Dayton finally see locally produced beer again?" it

Warped Wing Brewing repurposed this old foundry in downtown Dayton. *Author's collection.*

wondered. Within six years, nearly a score of small breweries and brewpubs were in business around the area.[103]

Craft beers are pricier than major domestic brands, but local brewers found no shortage of demand. It caught some by surprise. In 2013, unexpected success forced the Yellow Springs Brewery to shut down temporarily.

Unlike most other breweries, the Yellow Springs Brewery opened in a hard-to-find location in a small town that values community culture more than business growth. Co-owners Nate Cornett and his wife, Lisa Wolters, picked an out-of-the-way spot in a former seed company warehouse. It sat at the end of a long lane that once gave access to the Little Miami Railroad, long since converted to a paved recreational trail. Location wasn't crucial to them because they planned to brew mainly for distribution. They built a small, trail-facing taproom almost as an afterthought.

"We were open six weeks and ran out of beer. We had to close to brew more," Cornett said. Foot traffic streamed in from the trail. Wolters said the secluded location made the small brewery seem more special. "People started finding us, and they felt like it was their discovery, and they would tell their friends," she said. They expanded their taproom and replaced all their brewing equipment to boost capacity. By 2017, they were brewing four thousand barrels per year and had run out of space. They were converting an old bowling alley into a distribution center.[104]

The "Second Wave"

In 2018, local news media chronicled what one report termed a "second wave" of brewery openings across the region. Branch and Bone Artisan Ales opened that year in Dayton, and Devil Wind Brewing began serving in Xenia. Alematic Artisan Ales was in the planning stages in Huber Heights. Kettering-based Lock 27 opened a second brewery in downtown Dayton in late 2017. Up north, Moeller Brew Barn more than doubled its size in Maria Stein and was poised to open a satellite brewpub in a repurposed church in Troy.

Almost from the start, local observers wondered how much craft beer the Dayton region could absorb. "New brewpubs and microbreweries emerged as one of the hottest segments of the Miami Valley's retail economy in 2013. But will the craft beer trend go flat fast?" reporter Mark Fisher asked in a

Moeller Brew Barn opened in 2015 in rural Maria Stein. As of this writing, it was already expanding, with plans to open another brewpub in Troy. *Author's collection.*

2013 *Dayton Daily News* report. A third-generation Daytonian and thirty-year newspaper veteran, Fisher had covered Dayton's food and dining beat since 2006 and had seen many restaurants start up with great promise, only to fail after a few years. With the number of craft breweries more than doubling statewide in five years, Fisher wondered if the craft beer bubble was about to pop.

Five years later, it was still holding. "There's been no shakeout. None of the first wave or subsequent breweries has shut down. Nearly every single one of them has expanded in some way, most of them considerably. It's truly remarkable. And they leased space that no one wanted," he wrote in an e-mail in November 2018.[105]

Spurring Growth

As of this writing, the microbrewery trend was still strong, and the flourishing brewpubs were creating a number of spinoff benefits. Some took advantage of vacant commercial and industrial buildings in urban cores, and their taprooms dovetailed with municipal efforts to revitalize downtowns with entertainment. In downtown Dayton, for example, Warped Wing made its home in a vacant foundry, while Lock 27 repurposed an old General Motors Delco building. They added to the amenities for a downtown becoming increasingly popular with people seeking an urban lifestyle.

Beer tourism was another benefit, with two small tour companies in business as of this writing. The Dayton Ale Trail, created by nineteen local brewers with help from the Dayton Convention and Visitors Bureau, rewards participants who collect enough stamps in their "passport" books with a free jug of beer. Beer-themed festivals and special events are increasingly popular.

Small breweries with at least some ingredients grown in the Miami Valley reflect growing interest in local communities, according to Lock

Steve Barnhart, founder-owner of Lock 27, highlights Dayton's manufacturing history with touches such as beer taps mounted in an old welding tank. *Author's collection.*

27 owner and founder Steve Barnhart. "It's all about local in a lot of ways," Barnhart said in a 2017 interview. He started his first brewpub after spending two years commuting to a software job in Milwaukee following the departure of his former employer of twenty years, NCR Corporation. Dayton had suffered the loss of thousands of manufacturing jobs over many years, but the loss of NCR was an especially heavy blow. Dayton's sense of identity was closely bound to the homegrown Fortune 500 company. "For a long time, Dayton didn't have a lot to be proud of," Barnhart said. "As jobs left, they didn't come back. So now, coming out of that period and now into a period of growth, you can look at a brewery and say, 'That's my brewery. It's in my community.'"[106]

Importance of Local

Across the Dayton region, breweries have embraced their communities in different ways. Mother Stewart's buys its ingredients from local sources as much as possible, Kevin Loftis said. He said he was buying most of his brewery's honey, barley and even hops from within the region.

Other brewers around the state were also looking for local sources, rekindling demand for crops that once made up an important part of Ohio's agriculture industry. Meeting demand for hops has been especially challenging because the high-climbing plants take years to cultivate and are difficult to harvest. "We were major hops producers back before Prohibition. Probably every farm had some hops on them back in the old days," Brad Bergefurd, a horticultural specialist with the Ohio State University College of Agriculture, said in 2017.

To see how common hops once were, just walk or bike on the Little Miami Trail between Xenia and Yellow Springs in late summer. There, wild hop flowers can be found hanging like tiny green pine cones from vine-like bines snaking through the brush and trees along the trail. Bergefurd speculated they were the descendants of hop flowers that escaped from the freight cars of Little Miami Railroad trains as they hauled hops from farms to breweries.

But hop farming became a lost art in Ohio after Prohibition. When he started studying hops in 2012, Bergefurd knew of only three Ohio farms growing them, and they only amounted to a few acres. By 2017, he said, Ohio farmers were growing hops on about four hundred acres, but they

Wild hops grow along a recreation trail on the former Little Miami Railroad line, between Xenia and Yellow Springs. *Author's collection.*

were still nowhere near to meeting demand. "We need six thousand acres" to match what Ohio breweries were consuming that year, he said.

Jamie Arthur bought a small farm south of Xenia after a thirty-year career in financial management with computer and data companies. He grows the standard Ohio crops of corn and soybeans but also pumpkins, squash and specialty strains of barley and wheat. He added an acre of hops in 2014.

Arthur said the demand for local ingredients by nearby brewers was the only reason he bothered with hops. "If there were no craft brewers, we wouldn't try to grow them and sell them to Anheuser-Busch," he said.

Growing hops is labor intensive, but Arthur also found it gratifying. "The first time we sold the hops [to a local brewer] and they brewed beer with it, we went in there and had the beer. I knew then that was something I wanted to do," he said.[107]

Jamie Arthur, owner of Little Miami Farms south of Xenia, was one of several Ohio farmers growing hops and barley for local breweries as of this writing. *Author's collection.*

Brewers also teamed up with other local food producers to co-brand and cross-promote specialty items. Warped Wing, for example, collaborated with Esther Price Candies, a Dayton-based maker of fine chocolates since 1926, to make a seasonal brew dubbed Esther's Lil Secret. It makes each year's batch a surprise by changing the recipe.

Local brewers found they could turn to one another for help. When the Wandering Griffin Brewery and Pub opened in a former Quaker Steak & Lube restaurant in Beavercreek, it wasn't ready to brew its own beer. To fill the void, it worked with the Crooked Handle Brewing Company in Springboro to produce "Crooked Griffin," a New England–style IPA.

Glenn Perrine, who cofounded the Lucky Star Brewery and Cantina in Miamisburg with his wife, Ana, said the spirit of collaboration and even camaraderie they found among local brewpubs convinced them to dive into the business. "Instead of bad mouthing the other local breweries, they would give you directions and send you to visit them," he said in a 2016 *Akron Beacon Journal* interview. He credited the owners of Warped Wing Brewing with helping him learn the trade.[108]

TIES TO HISTORY

In identifying with their local communities, some craft brewers have also drawn on local history to brand themselves and their products. Warped Wing's name is a nod to the Wright brothers' breakthrough invention, a method of controlling an airplane by warping its wings. Its Ermal's Belgian Style Cream Ale is named for the late Ermal Fraze, a local tool company owner who invented the easy-opening beverage can. In Springfield, Devil Wind Brewing draws its name from Xenia's history of deadly tornadoes, and its Hollencamp Helles Lager memorializes the family of brewers who came before it.

Steve Barnhart decided to tie his brewpub to Dayton's canal history, so he named it after the part of the canal closest to his first location: Lock 27, a restored canal lock south of Miamisburg. Barnhart said a tie to a community's history helps reinforce the notion it's a homegrown business with local products. "It's all about local in a lot of ways, so for us to hit on that history, it's just about reinforcing that sense of local. I think we all come to it from that perspective," he said.

The Dayton History organization brought the region's brewing heritage to life with its authentic, 1850s-style Carillon Brewing brewpub and restaurant. *Dayton History.*

As of this writing, the Miami Valley's craft beer industry is beginning to reflect what brewing and drinking were like more than a century ago, before Dayton's brewers consolidated and before local option elections across the region set the stage for Prohibition. In those days, most locally owned breweries served their local communities, while a few distributed more widely. Beer lovers knew their brewers.

Prohibition, the Great Depression and the rise of national brands seemed to wipe away all but the barest hints of the industry as it once was. But it's a part of the region's history that deserves to be remembered, as do the people who made it.

CRAFT BREWERIES TODAY

The Miami Valley's craft beer scene is rapidly growing and changing as of this writing. The numbers and styles of beers vary and may include ciders and non-alcoholic beverages. A few breweries also make wine. Several distribute beers in cans or bottles. The descriptions of all breweries in this section reflect their status in early 2019. Please visit their websites for current information.

Tailspin Brewing repurposed this old dairy barn, preserving a local landmark in Coldwater. *Author's collection.*

CLARK COUNTY

MOTHER STEWART'S BREWING
109 West North Street, Springfield 45504
motherstewartsbrewing.com

Mother Stewart's Brewing is a production brewery in downtown Springfield. It's named after Eliza Daniel "Mother" Stewart, an important temperance crusader who lived in Springfield. The brewery, its 8,500-square-foot taproom and a large outdoor beer garden are located in the former Springfield Metallic Casket Company. Its website advertises ten varieties of beer.

PINUPS AND PINTS
10963 Lower Valley Pike, Medway 45341
pinupsandpints.com

Pinups and Pints bills itself as "the world's only strip club–brew pub." It has a fifteen-gallon brewing system and offers a single India pale ale.

GREENE COUNTY

DEVIL WIND BREWING
130 South Detroit Street, Xenia 45385
devilwindbrewing.com

Devil Wind Brewing occupies a former industrial building less than half a mile from the site of the old Hollencamp brewery. It takes its name from Xenia's history of destructive tornadoes, but one of its first brews, Hollencamp Helles Lager, paid tribute to Xenia's brewing heritage. Its facility includes a three-thousand-square-foot taproom and a small patio with six beers on tap.

YELLOW SPRINGS BREWERY
305 North Walnut Street, Suite B, Yellow Springs 45387
yellowspringsbrewery.com

Yellow Springs Brewery is a production brewery in a former seed company warehouse, but its trailside taproom and patio have made it a popular destination for craft beer lovers on foot or bicycle. Its beer lineup includes five core brands on tap, seven packaged and fourteen in seasonal rotations.

MERCER COUNTY (CLOSEST BREWERIES TO AUGLAIZE, DARKE AND SHELBY COUNTIES)

MOELLER BREW BARN
8016 Marion Drive, Maria Stein 45860
moellerbrewbarn.com

Situated in a small village surrounded by farmland, Moeller Brew Barn is a production brewery with a taproom, kitchen and outdoor patio. It offers seventeen beers. It's expanding its production capacity to 4,500 barrels per year, with room to grow to 7,000, enlarging its taproom and adding a kitchen. In Troy, it's renovating an old church at 214 West Main Street for a satellite production brewery and taproom.

TAILSPIN BREWING
626 South Second Street, Coldwater 45828
tailspinbrewing.co

Tailspin is a small, veteran-owned brewpub reflecting owner and founder Jack Waite's years as a U.S. Air Force officer and fighter pilot. It occupies a picturesque, 1933 dairy barn. The taproom includes an upstairs party room and a balcony patio. It offers thirteen house beers.

Montgomery County

Alematic Artisan Ales
6182 Chambersburg Road, Huber Heights 45424
alematicbrewing.com

The newest brewery as of this writing, Alematic is a four-thousand-square-foot brewery and taproom offering eight house beers.

Branch and Bone Artisan Ales
905 Wayne Avenue, Dayton 45410
branchandboneales.com

Branch and Bone is a very small brewpub in a repurposed commercial building in Dayton's historic South Park neighborhood, two blocks from where Michael Schiml introduced Dayton to lager beer. It specializes in unconventional brews, including mixed fermentation styles as well as spontaneous fermentation. It has a dozen house beers on tap.

Carillon Brewing
1000 Carillon Boulevard, Dayton 45409
carillonbrewingco.org

Located in Dayton History's Carillon Historical Park, Carillon Brewing is a faithful rendition of an 1850s Dayton brewery, built with brick and timber-frame construction. Its house beers are brewed with traditional recipes, ingredients and methods, including open kettles over wood fires and fermentation in oak barrels. Brewers and servers wear period costumes. For a fee, one can be "brewer for a day," working as apprentice to the head brewer. Its restaurant offers dishes that would have been available locally in the mid-1800s. Besides a few traditionally brewed house beers, wine, cider and root beer, it offers several commercial brands and local craft beers. Separate from the restaurant, its eighty-seat Bier Hall can be rented for special events.

CROOKED HANDLE BREWING
760 North Main Street, Springboro 45066
crookedhandle.com

Counties to the south of Montgomery lie beyond the scope of this book. Crooked Handle is in northern Warren County, but it serves a population straddling the county line. The small storefront brewpub sells mainly in its taproom but also cans individual beers on a rotating basis. It offers eleven house beers, plus a few from around the region, with some from an experimental brewing club it hosts.

THE DAYTON BEER COMPANY
41 Madison Street, Dayton 45431
thedaytonbeerco.com

The Dayton Beer Company started with a small pilot brewery in 2010. It opened a brewpub in Kettering in May 2012. In April 2015, it opened a production brewery and taproom in downtown Dayton, and in 2017, it closed its original Kettering location. The downtown location features a large, bier hall–style taproom and a large outdoor beer garden. It offers a large number of regional and house beers, with some seasonal and some in rotation.

EUDORA BREWING
3022 Wilmington Pike, Kettering 45429
eudorabrewing.com

Eudora Brewing opened as a small, storefront brewpub in a strip mall. In early 2019, it moved into a standalone building with a twenty-thousand-square-foot brewpub and kitchen as well as a private event room. For a fee, customers can brew their own small batches using Eudora's equipment and bottle it for home consumption. It offers nine year-round and seven seasonal beers.

FIFTH STREET BREWPUB
1600 East Fifth Street, Dayton 45403
fifthstreetbrewpub.coop

Fifth Street Brewpub features a tavern, restaurant and large beer garden operated by a nonprofit cooperative. It revitalized a vacant corner market built in 1860 in the historic Saint Anne's Hill neighborhood. It boasts more than 3,200 member-owners, but it's also open to the public. Its taps serve seven house beers and four from around Ohio and neighboring states.

HAIRLESS HARE BREWERY
738 West National Road, Vandalia 45377
hairlessharebrewery.com

Hairless Hare is a storefront brewery in a retail plaza across U.S. 40 from the Dayton International Airport. It serves pizza, hamburgers and appetizers along with nine house and one or more regional beers.

HEAVIER THAN AIR BREWING
497 Miamisburg-Centerville Road, Centerville 45459
heavierthanairbrewing.com

The name Heavier than Air Brewing refers to the heavier-than-air flying machine invented by the Wright brothers and reflects the aviation passion of cofounder Chris Tarkany, a private pilot. The small brewery and taproom occupy a unit of a strip mall in suburban Washington Township. It offers six year-round and seven seasonal or rotating beers.

LOCK 27 BREWING
Dayton Brewery & Pub: Dayton Dragons Plaza, 329 East First Street (rear), Dayton 45402
Centerville Brewpub: 1035 South Main Street, Centerville 45458
lock27brewing.com

Named for the nearest Miami and Erie Canal lock to its original Centerville location, Lock 27 draws on the region's history and innovative spirit. Its main brewpub occupies an old General Motors Delco industrial building, which has a First Street address but opens onto the Dayton Dragons baseball stadium plaza. Its menu ranges from brunch to dinner entrées. It offers five house beers with suggested food pairings. Its pub reinforces the building's industrial heritage with architectural touches, such as taps mounted in an old welding tank. Since opening in Dayton, its Centerville brewpub has become the place where it tests new beers and offers dishes from an "eclectic" kitchen.

LUCKY STAR BREWERY AND CANTINA
219 South Second Street, Miamisburg 45342
luckystarbrewery.com

Lucky Star occupies an early 1800s factory building in Miamisburg's historic neighborhood. The rough industrial texture of the three-story, brick building is softened by a Mexican cantina theme, including boldly colored trim and whimsical décor. It rotates a variety of house and other Ohio beers, but its flagship beer is Ojos Locos, a pale lager. Its small kitchen offers Mexican dishes. Its brewing tanks are the centerpiece of its main taproom. It also has an outdoor patio.

STAR CITY BREWING
319 South Second Street, Miamisburg 45342
starcitybrewing.com

Miamisburg's first brewery in more than a century, Star City Brewing revived a long-vacant building that once housed the Peerless Mill Inn, a popular downtown restaurant. It was originally a sawmill built in 1828 along the Miami and Erie Canal. Its main taproom is a rustic tavern with wood beams, a stone floor and a fireplace, but the sprawling facility offers a game room, a patio and large spaces available for private events. It offers eleven house brands and its own wine.

TOXIC BREW
431 East Fifth Street, Dayton 45402
toxicbrewcompany.com

Toxic Brew's owners repurposed a pawn shop in Dayton's historic Oregon District to open the city's first brewery in half a century. Its small taproom's brick walls reflect the texture of the neighborhood's brick streets and buildings. Its two batteries of double-decker taps include twenty house beers and others from surrounding states. It has a small canning operation but is planning a separate production brewery.

WANDERING GRIFFIN BREWERY AND PUB
3725 Presidential Drive, Beavercreek 45324
wanderinggriffin.com

Wandering Griffin opened its Beavercreek brewpub without a brewery. It brews four house brands in collaboration with three other local breweries and offers numerous beers, wines and bourbons from around the country. It's building a seven-barrel brewing system. Located in a former restaurant, its kitchen offers a full menu.

WARPED WING BREWING
26 Wyandot Street, Dayton 45402
warpedwing.com

Warped Wing opened its production brewery and taproom in the former Buckeye Iron and Glassworks Foundry. The surrounding neighborhood is steeped in brewing history, close to the former Sachs Pruden building and the area where James Riddle had a brewery in 1840 or earlier. Warped Wing named its Superba pilsner for the former Olt Brewing Company's once-popular brand. It offers five year-round beers, a dozen seasonals and frequent special release. It distributes in cans and bottles.

NOTES

Introduction

1. Author interview with Kyle Spears, November 30, 2018.

Chapter 1

2. George W. Knepper, *The Official Ohio Lands Book* (Columbus, OH: Auditor of State, 2002), 1–2, 6, 12, https://ohioauditor.gov/publications/OhioLandsBook.pdf; Robert W. Steele and Mary Davies Steele, *Early Dayton* (Dayton, OH: U.B. Publishing House, 1896), 20–21, 30, 32, 51, 53, 96–97; A.W. Drury, *History of the City of Dayton and Montgomery County, Ohio*, vols. 1 and 2 (Chicago: S.J. Clarke, 1909), 1:72–75, 76, 111, 132.

3. Frank Conover, ed., *Centennial Portrait and Biographical Record of the City of Dayton and Montgomery County, Ohio* (Dayton, OH: A.W. Bowen & Company, 1897), 573, 801; W.A. Shuey, *Historical and Statistical Tables Relating to the City of Dayton, Ohio, 1749–1896* (Dayton, OH: United Brethren Publishing House, 1896), 221; will of John W. Harries, *Ohio Wills and Probate Records, 1786–1998*, Ancestry.com, https://www.ancestry.com/interactive/8801/005876877_00350/11584867; Steele and Steele, *Early Dayton*, 152; Alvin F. Harlow, *Old Towpaths: The Story of the American Canal*

Era (Port Washington, NY: D. Appleton & Company, 1926), 241; Robert A. Musson, *Brewing Beer in the Gem City: A Pictorial History of the Brewing Industry in Dayton, Ohio* (Medina, OH: Zepp Publications, 2014), 4.

4. "Death of James Riddle," *Dayton Journal*, August 24, 1855, 2; "Death of Mrs. Isabella Riddle," *Dayton Journal*, April 27, 1875, 4; W.H. Beers, *The History of Montgomery County, Ohio* (Chicago: W.H. Beers & Company, 1882), Book 2, 598; Book 3, 207–8, 420; Harvey W. Crew, *History of Dayton, Ohio, with Portraits and Biographical Sketches of Some of Its Pioneer and Prominent Citizens* (Dayton, OH: United Brethren Publishing House, 1889), 441–42; affidavit of Henry Ferneding, February 10, 1900, Montgomery County, Ohio, Deed Book 235, page 13, County Recorder's Office, Dayton, Ohio; Conover, *Centennial Portrait*, 755; "Clement J. Ferneding—Pioneer Citizen," location sign, Calvary Cemetery, Kettering, Ohio, n.d.

5. Stephen Yool and Andrew Comrie, "A Taste of Place: Environmental Geographies of the Classic Beer Styles," in *The Geography of Beer: Regions, Environment and Societies*, ed. Mark Patterson and Nancy Pullen (New York: Springer Science & Business Media, 2014), 70, 74; "America's First Lager," Pennsylvania State Historical Marker, n.d., http://explorepahistory.com/hmarker.php?markerId=1-A-31C.

6. Library of Congress, "A New Surge of Growth," https://www.loc.gov/teachers/classroommaterials/presentationsandactivities/presentations/immigration/alt/german4.html; Library of Congress, "Chronology," The Germans in America, April 23, 2014, https://www.loc.gov/rr/european/imde/germchro.html; Beers, *History of Montgomery County*, Book 3, 24; Rich Exner, "Percent German and Irish for Each Ohio City: Census Estimates," Cleveland.com, December 29, 2016, https://www.cleveland.com/datacentral/index.ssf/2016/12/percent_german_and_irish_for_e.html; Samuel A. Batzli, "Mapping United States Breweries 1612 to 2011," in *Geography of Beer*, 34–36; Frederick William Salem, *Beer, Its History and Its Economic Value as a National Beverage* (Hartford, CT: F.W. Salem & Company, 1880), 189–90, 240–46, https://books.google.com/books?id=bLlBAQAAMAAJ; Annie Wittenmyer, *History of the Woman's Temperance Crusade* (Philadelphia, PA: Christian Woman, 1878), 323–24, https://catalog.hathitrust.org/Record/001133563.

7. Beers, *History of Montgomery County*, Book 3, 238–39; Robert Wahl and Max Henius, eds., *Brewers' Guide 1896* (Chicago: Der Braumeister Publishing Company, 1896), 64, https://digitalcollections.nypl.org/items/ce2c48e0-cf10-0131-e663-58d385a7b928; Robert Wahl and Max Henius, *Brewers'*

Guide 1898 (Chicago: American Brewers' Review Company, 1898), 67, https://digitalcollections.nypl.org/items/54b8d330-cf0f-0131-98c1-58d385a7bbd0; Crew, *History of Dayton*, 425–26; "Brewery Deal," *Dayton Daily News*, August 20, 1900, 7; "Dayton Beer Barons," *Dayton Daily Journal*, Monday, April 24, 1893, 3.

8. Emmanuel Catholic Church, "Church History," http://www.emmanuelcatholic.com/about/history-of-emmanuel; "Funeral of the Late Titus Schwind," *Dayton Journal*, January 27, 1879, 4; "Dayton Beer Barons," *Dayton Daily Journal*, 3.

9. Beers, *History of Montgomery County*, Book 3, 239–40, 243; "Funeral of the Late Titus Schwind," *Dayton Daily Journal*, January 27, 1879, 4; "Died Suddenly in a Street Car," *Dayton Daily Journal*, December 23, 1907, 1; "Found Dead in Her Bed," *Dayton Journal*, June 13, 1885, 4.

10. "United States Census, 1850," Brookville, Indiana, FamilySearch https://familysearch.org/ark:/61903/3:1:S3HT-69RQ-D4T; "United States Census, 1870," Ward 8, Dayton, Ohio, FamilySearch, https://familysearch.org/ark:/61903/3:1:S3HT-6DHS-TY9.

11. Cynthia G. Fox, "Income Tax Records of the Civil War Years," *Prologue Magazine* 18, no. 4 (Winter 1986), https://www.archives.gov/publications/prologue/1986/winter/civil-war-tax-records.html; Ohio History Connection, "Correspondence to the Governor and Adjutant General, 1861–1866," *Civil War Guide Project* (Columbus: Ohio History Connection), n.d., http://resources.ohiohistory.org/onlinedoc/civilwar/civilwar-new.php; Historical Data Systems, "U.S. Civil War Soldier Records and Profiles, 1861–1865," Ancestry, https://search.ancestry.com/cgi-bin/sse.dll?indiv=1&dbid=1555&h=82805.

12. Drury, *History of the City of Dayton*, 1:234; Crew, *History of Dayton, Ohio*, 656; "Dayton Beer Barons," *Dayton Daily Journal*, 3; Sanborn, *Insurance Maps of Dayton, Ohio* (New York: Sanborn Map & Publishing Company Ltd.), *1887*, map 25; *1897*, map 67. Note that the Sanborn maps consulted for this work were in the Ohio Public Library Information Network's online database, https://oh0063.oplin.org:2172/viewer/?id=15683. An OPLIN member library card was required.

13. Martin J. Kelly, "Memory of Mansion Replaces Horizon House," *Dayton Daily News*, December 6, 1986, n.p.; "Corporation Record," *National Corporation Reporter*, January 16, 1892, 374, https://books.google.com/books?id=cpNDAQAAMAAJ&pg=PA374.

14. Conover, *Centennial Portrait*, 755–56; "The Plan Under Which the Schwind Brewery Reorganized," *Dayton Daily News*, June 22, 1900, 7; "Schwind

Brewing Co.," *Dayton Daily News*, May 31, 1902, 27; "Schwind Realty Co. Is Incorporated," *Dayton Daily News*, March 29, 1907, 12.

15. Schwind Building advertisement, *Dayton Daily News*, December 14, 1912, 13; "Michael Schwind Called by Death," *Dayton Journal*, December 9, 1907, 1.

16. Kelly, "Memory of Mansion"; *SC-74 Jane Reece Studio Collection, ca 1924* (Fairborn, OH: Wright State University Special Collections and Archives, n.d.); Jack Anderson, "Josephine Schwarz, 95, Leader in Growth of Regional Ballets," *New York Times*, March 2, 2018, n.p.; "Dayton Beer Barons," *Dayton Daily Journal*, 3.

Chapter 2

17. "Adam Schantz Is No More," *Dayton Daily News*, April 21, 1903, 11; "Dayton Beer Barons," *Dayton Daily Journal*, 3; marriage record for Frederick Schantz and Barbara Olt, "Ohio, County Marriage Records, 1774–1993," Ancestry, https://www.ancestry.com/interactive/61378/TH-1-18084-97809-10; "Obituary," *American Brewers' Review*, May 20, 1903, 522–23.

18. "Obituary," *American Brewers' Review*, May 20, 1903, 522–23; Crew, *History of Dayton, Ohio*, 431–32; Shuey, *Historical and Statistical Tables*, 221.

19. Drury, *History of the City of Dayton*, 2:596–97; "Corporation Record," *National Corporation Reporter*, May 26, 1894, 244; Wahl and Henius, *Brewers' Guide*, 1896, 65.

20. "Oldest Dayton Hotel Man and Pioneer Resident Dead," *Dayton Daily News*, February 22, 1909, 6; "Brewery Deal," *Dayton Daily News*, August 20, 1900, 7; "Corporation Affairs," *American Brewers' Review*, September 20, 1900, 97.

21. Drury, *History of the City of Dayton*, 2:432–36, 596–97; Beers, *History of Montgomery County*, Book 2, 631; "Brave Millwright Risked His Life," *Dayton Daily News*, December 5, 1901, 10; "Fine Quality Is the Wall," *Dayton Daily News*, December 20, 1902, C5.

22. Beers, *History of Montgomery County*, Book 2, 631; Book 3, 24; Stickle's advertisement, *Dayton Daily News*, June 20, 1899, 23; "Citizen Dies of Old Age," *Dayton Daily News*, November 21, 1908, 2.

23. Conover, *Centennial Portrait*, 595–96; Wahl and Henius, *Brewers' Guide*, 1898, 67, 69; "Incorporated Companies," *Williams' Dayton Directory for 1909–1910* (Cincinnati, OH: Williams' Directory Company, 1909), 51;

"Theodore Hollencamp," *Dayton Daily News*, June 22, 1901, 5; "Head of Dayton Brewery Dies," *Dayton Daily Journal*, January 1, 1936, 1.

24. Beers, *History of Montgomery County*, Book 3, 393, 631; Drury, *History of Dayton*, 2:972–73; Crew, *History of Dayton*, 454; Indiana Historical Bureau, "Canal Construction in Indiana," *Indiana Historian*, September 1997, 10, https://www.in.gov/history/files/canalconstruction.pdf.

25. "Nicholas Thomas, Self-Made Man of Prominence, Expires," *Dayton Daily Journal*, August 23, 1913, 1; "$75,000 Addition to Be Erected," *Dayton Daily News*, October 1, 1901, 10.

26. J. Fletcher Brennan, ed., *A Biographical Cyclopædia of Distinguished Men, with an Historical Sketch of the State of Ohio, Part 3* (Cincinnati, OH: John C. Yorston & Company, 1879), 450–51; Crew, *History of Dayton*, 407; "Dayton Beer Barons," *Dayton Daily Journal*, 3; "Receivers Report Desired," *Dayton Daily News*, March 29, 1899, 5; "Mr. Edward Sachs for Fifty Years a Resident of Dayton Is Dead," *Dayton Daily News*, July 3, 1901, 1; "Paralytic Stroke," *Dayton Daily News*, January 16, 1899, 2.

27. Anheuser-Busch, "An Ambitious Legacy," *Budweiser* (St. Louis, MO: Anheuser-Busch Companies, n.d.), https://www.budweiser.com/en/our-legacy.html; "Schantz Letter," *Dayton Daily News*, December 14, 1900, 2.

28. "Real Estate Deal," *Dayton Daily News*, July 16, 1900, 5; advertisement for Schlitz Palm and Roof Garden, *Dayton Daily News*, July 20, 1901, 8; University of Wisconsin–Milwaukee Libraries, postcard, "Schlitz Palm Garden, Milwaukee," *Greetings from Milwaukee: Selections from the Thomas and Jean Ross Bliffert Postcard Collection* (Milwaukee: University of Wisconsin–Milwaukee Libraries, n.d.), https://collections.lib.uwm.edu/digital/collection/gfmmke/id/701; "A Towering Giant," *Dayton Daily News*, May 31, 1902, 26.

29. Oakwood Historical Society, *Schantz Park*, 3–4; Dale P. Van Wieren, ed., "Chronology of the American Brewing Industry," excerpted from *American Breweries II* (Cleveland, OH: Eastern Coast Breweriana Association, 1995), http://www.beerhistory.com/library/holdings/chronology.shtml.

30. "Adam Schantz Is President," *Dayton Daily News*, March 1, 1904, 7; "Big Brewery Deal Formally Closed," *Dayton Daily News*, September 29, 1906, 4; "Suite of Rooms in the Arcade," *Dayton Daily News*, February 6, 1904, 10; "Beautifully Dedicated by a Labor of Charity," *Dayton Daily News*, March 3, 1904, 1; "Many Saloons Will Be Closed," *Dayton Daily News*, March 2, 1904, 3; "When Herrick Signs Measure 'Twill Be a Law," *Dayton Daily News*, April 16, 4.

31. "Olt Brewing Company," *Dayton Daily News*, November 7, 1906, page 9; "Site Secured for the New Brewery," *Dayton Daily News*, November 19, 1906, 11; "Dayton Breweries," *Greenville (OH) Journal*, February 21, 1907, 2.

Chapter 3

32. "Miami Valley Brewery Fire," *Miamisburg Bulletin*, March 29, 1889, 1.
33. Author interview with Justin Kohnen, November 29, 2018; Henry Howe, *Historical Collections of Ohio*, vol. 2 (Cincinnati, OH: C.J. Krehbiel & Company, 1902), 299; advertisement, *Miamisburg Bulletin*, December 27, 1867, 1.
34. Deed of sale from John Harman to Phillip Harman and Margaret Nusz, August 18, 1860, County Recorder's Office, Dayton, OH, Deed Book I3, page 537.
35. "Miamisburg," *Dayton Daily Journal*, August 3, 1881, 4.
36. Sanborn, *Miamisburg, Ohio, April 1886*, map 5; *April 1892*, map 5; "Miami Valley Brewery Fire," *Miamisburg Bulletin*, March 21, 1889, 1; Samuel M. Taylor, *Annual Report of the Secretary of State to the Governor of the State of Ohio for the Year Ending November 15, 1894* (Columbus, OH: Westbote Company, 1895), 470.
37. Conover, *Centennial Portrait*, 975–76; Stephen D. Cone, *A Concise History of Hamilton, Ohio* (Middletown, OH: George Mitchell, 1901), 229, 340, 406–7; "Miamisburg," *Dayton Daily News*, August 29, 1899, 2.
38. "Frigiferous Particulars," *Ice and Refrigeration Illustrated* (March 1898): 193, https://books.google.com/books?id=SuFBAQAAMAAJ; "Artificial Ice," *Miamisburg News*, August 3, 1889, 1; "A Big Fire," *Miamisburg News*, May 10, 1900, 1; "Disastrous Fire in Miamisburg," *Dayton Daily News*, May 8, 1990, 1.

Chapter 4

39. M.A. Broadstone, ed., *History of Greene County, Ohio, Its People, Industries and Institutions*, vol. 1 (Indianapolis, IN: B.F. Bowen & Company, 1918), 703; Marilyn Shannon, "Hollencamp House," *Ohio Historic Inventory* (Columbus: Ohio Historical Society, December 7, 1972); L.H. Everts & Company, *Combination Atlas Map of Greene County, Ohio* (Chicago: L.H. Everts & Company, 1874), 41.

40. Wittenmyer, *History*, 258–62; Mary F. Eastman, *Biography of Dio Lewis* (New York: Fowler & Wells, 1891), 218–19, https://books.google.com/books?id=J67qXsLvJOQC; George T. Ferris, *Minnie Hermon; or, the Curse of Rum* (New York: Henry S. Goodspeed & Company, 1878), 535, https://books.google.com/books?id=yVxGAAAAYAAJ.

41. Wahl and Henius, *Brewers' Guide*, 1896, 66; 1898, 67; news briefs, *Xenia Daily Gazette*, July 7, 1885, n.p.; September 14, 1885, n.p.; December 9, 1889, n.p.; April 22, 1897, n.p.

42. Union B. Hunt, "Articles of Association," *Report of the Secretary of State* (Indianapolis, IN: William B. Burford, 1900), 133, https://books.google.com/books?id=szsbAQAAIAAJ; "Requiem Mass for D.J. Hollencamp Will Be Saturday," *Xenia Daily Gazette*, June 19, 1941, n.p.; "Went Dry Against Odds," *Dayton Daily News*, September 4, 1901, 7.

43. "New Ice Machine," *Xenia Gazette*, January 9, 1902, n.p.; news brief, *Xenia Gazette and Torchlight*, August 20, 1903, n.p.; "Corporation Affairs," *American Brewers' Review*, September 20, 1903, 108, https://books.google.com/books?id=5tpOAAAAYAAJ; "Bishop Fallows' 'Home Salon,'" *Homiletic Review*, September 1895, 282, https://books.google.com/books?id=BrMnAAAAYAAJ.

44. "Sewers Flushed with Beer, *New York Sun*, July 1, 1905, 1.

45. James C. Oda, "Piqua Has Place in Pages of Brewing History," *Piqua Daily Call*, September 21, 1991, n.p.; "Bungs," *The Western Brewer*, February 1909, 108, https://books.google.com/books?id=eOs1AQAAMAAJ; Thomas Bemis Wheeler, *Troy: The Nineteenth Century* (Troy, OH: Troy Historical Society, 1970), 283.

46. W.H. Beers, *The History of Miami County, Ohio* (Chicago: W.H. Beers & Company, 1880), 701–2; "Titus Schwind," Ohio Wills and Probate Records, 1786–1998, Montgomery County, https://www.ancestry.com/interactive/8801/005876877_00869?pid=11584518. Note: Some ancestry databases incorrectly indexed Titus Schwind as "Silas Schind."

47. Death record for George Mayer, Ohio, County Death Records, 1840–2001, Miami Death Records, 1894–1908, vols. 3–4, frame 206, FamilySearch, https://familysearch.org/ark:/61903/3:1:3QSQ-G9ZB-29F2-4; Emilius O. Randall and Daniel J. Ryan, *History in Ohio: The Rise and Progress of an American State* (New York: Century History Company, 1912), 459.

48. "Miami County Voted 'Dry' by Good-Sized Majority," *Dayton Daily News*, November 25, 1908, 4; "Amber Fluid Flows Freely; Many Drunk," *Dayton Daily News*, April 23, 1909, 19.

Chapter 5

49. John A. Rayner, *The First Century of Piqua, Ohio* (Piqua, OH: Magee Brothers Publishing Company, 1916), 16–17, 232; L.H. Everts & Company, *Illustrated Historical Atlas of Miami County, Ohio* (Philadelphia, PA: L.H. Everts & Company, 1875), 9.

50. Ibid., 54, 61, 232.

51. F. Edgar, *Pioneer Life in Dayton and Vicinity, 1796–1840* (Dayton, OH: U.S. Publishing House, 1896), 217–18; "Gideon B. Beall," Conyers Family Tree, Ancestry, https://www.ancestry.com/family-tree/person/tree/12071960/person/842172227/facts; W.H. McIntosh, *The History of Darke County, Ohio* (Chicago: W.H. Beers & Company, 1880), 538–39; "Washington A. Weston & Wife Elizabeth to J. Lewis Schneyer," Miami County Recorder's Office, Troy, Ohio, August 29, 1851, Deed Book 18: 739–40, 26: 546–47.

52. Rayner, *First Century of Piqua*, 83; Harlow, *Old Towpaths*, 256, 258.

53. Beers, *History of Miami County*, 450; "Heartman Ploch to Butcher & Mittler," Miami County Recorder's Office, Troy, Ohio, December 1, 1879, Lease Book 60, page 185; Salem, *Beer*, 245.

54. "Henry Schneider: Well Known Brewer Passes Away After Long Illness," *Piqua Leader Dispatch*, November 19, 1903, n.p.; "Henry Schneider, Brewery," *General Business Review of Miami County, 1890*, n.p.; "Henry Schneider," *Piqua Journal and Daily Dispatch*, March 3, 1896, n.p.

55. "Capt. L. Kiefer Lost a Brave Fight," *Piqua Daily Call*, December 1, 1903, n.p.; Jeff Suess, *Lost Cincinnati* (Charleston, SC: The History Press, 2015), 137; Rayner, *First Century of Piqua*, 176; Salem, *Beer*, 245.

56. Rayner, *First Century of Piqua*, 97; Wahl and Henius, *Brewers' Guide*, 1896, 66; 1898, 68; Sanborn, *Insurance Maps of Piqua, 1905*, map 15.

57. "J.L. Schneyer, Brewery, No. 201 Spring Street," *General Business Review of Miami County*," 1890, n.p.; biographical sketch of Fred J. Lange, Citizens Historical Association, Indianapolis, Indiana, 1940, in Lange Document Collection, Local History Department, Piqua Public Library; "Lange Brewery Bottling Plant Opens Next Week," *Piqua Daily Call*, July 13, 1936, n.p.; U.S. Census Bureau, "History," https://www.census.gov/history/www/genealogy/decennial_census_records/availability_of_1890_census.html.

58. A.B.C. Hitchcock, *History of Shelby County, Ohio and Representative Citizens* (Chicago: Richmond-Arnold Publishing Company, 1913), 192, 573; John C. Hover et al., eds., *Memoirs of the Miami Valley*, vol. 3 (Chicago: Robert

O. Law Company, 1919), 485; R. Sutton, *History of Shelby County, Ohio* (Philadelphia, PA: R. Sutton & Company, 1883), 385; "Thirsty Line River Banks," *Dayton Daily News*, January 23, 1909, 5; "Bungs," *The Western Brewer* (Chicago: Gibson Publishing Company, February 1909), 108, https://books.google.com/books?id=eOs1AQAAMAAJ&pg=PA108.

59. "Fire and Accident Record," *Industrial Ice and Refrigeration*, March 1893, 206, https://books.google.com/books?id=0BRGAQAAMAA.

60. "Company Meetings and Elections," *American Brewers' Review*, March 1914, 111; March 1915, 113.

61. Richard H. Wallace, *Voices from the Past*, vol. 2 (Sidney, OH: Shelby County Historical Society, 2003), 274; Aspen Family Center, "Who We Are," http://aspenfamilycenter.com; John C. Hover, et al., eds, *Memoirs of the Miami Valley*, vol. 1 (Chicago: Robert O. Law Company, 1919), 485, https://books.google.com/books?id=STwVAAAAYAAJ&pg=PA485.

Chapter 6

62. ODNR Division of Wildlife, "Grand Lake St. Marys," http://wildlife.ohiodnr.gov/grandlakestmarys.

63. Author interview with Nick Moeller, October 15, 2017.

64. Ohio History Central, "German Ohioans," http://www.ohiohistory central.org/w/German_Ohioans.

65. Louis A., Rita and David Hoying, *Pilgrims All: A History of Saint Augustine Parish* (Minster, OH: St. Augustine Parish, 1982), 2, 13, 49–50; Clifford Neal Smith, *Early Nineteenth-Century German Settlers in Ohio (Mainly Cincinnati and Environs), Kentucky, and Other States* (Baltimore, MD: Genealogical Publishing Company, 2004), 48–50, originally published McNeal, AZ: Westland Publications, 1984–91, https://books.google.com/books?id=Pz0Pla3lXyQC; Census Office, *Report on Population of the United States* (Washington, D.C.: Government Printing Office, 1895), 386; C.A.O. McClellan and C.S. Warner, *Map of Auglaize County, Ohio* (Newton, CT: C.S. Warner, n.d.), http://hdl.loc.gov/loc.gmd/g4083a.la000600. Note: The Library of Congress dates the map as "186-" (sometime in the 1860s).

66. Salem, *Beer*, 244; "Veteran Minster Brewmaster Presides at Vats for 51 Years," *Lima News*, February 20, 1935, 5; H.G. Howland, *Atlas of Auglaize County, Ohio* (Philadelphia, OH: Robt. Sutton, 1880), 33; "Henry Lange, Deceased," *Brewers Journal*, March 1909, 140, https://books.google.com/books?id=eOs1AQAAMAAJ; "Mr. Frank Herkenhoff," *Minster*

Post, October 25, 1918, 1; biographical sketch of Fred J. Lange; William J. McMurray, ed., *History of Auglaize County, Ohio*, vol. 2 (Indianapolis, IN: Historical Publishing Company, 1923), 216–17; "Brewing Was Big Business," *Sidney Daily News*, October 2, 1982, 1; "Minster Brewery Marks 70th Anniversary Year," *Minster Post*, June 23, 1939, 1, 8; "Veteran Minster Brewmaster Presides at Vats for 51 Years," *Lima (OH) News*, February 20, 1935, 1, 5.

67. Wahl and Henius, *Brewers' Guide, 1896*, 66; "American Brewing Academy," *American Brewers' Review*, 474, https://books.google.com/books?id=Xn5PAAAAYAAJ; "Joseph Brinkman Rites Conducted Here Tuesday," *Minster Post*, October 15, 1943, 1; "Minster Brewery Marks 70th Anniversary Year," *Minster Post*, June 23, 1939, 1.

68. "Veteran Minster Brewmaster," *Lima News*; "Deaths and Funerals," *Lima (OH) News*, January 17, 1940, 4; "Civic Association Tours Old Wooden Shoe Brewery," *Community Post*, June 9, 1983, n.p.; Precision Strip, "History Timeline," https://www.precision-strip.com/about-us/history-timeline.

69. Margie Wuebker, "Brewing It Again," *Celina (OH) Daily Standard*, September 24, 2010., n.p.; Rick Armon, "Wooden Shoe R.I.P.," *Akron Beacon Journal*/Ohio.com, September 16, 2012, https://www.ohio.com/akron/pages/wooden-shoe-r-i-p; "Charles Koch, Director of the Boston Beer Company, Dies at 88," news release, Boston Beer Company Inc., June 15, 2011.

70. Howland, *Atlas* (1880), 31; Salem, *Beer*, 245; "Henry Schwers Spits Out Bullet," *The Towpath*, New Bremen Historic Association, http://www.newbremenhistory.org/Schwers,Hy.-bullet.htm.

71. Howland, *Atlas* (1880), 41; Walsh, *Atlas* (1898), 33.

72. Sanborn, *Wapakoneta, July 1885*, map 3; *November 1892*, map 4; Wahl and Henius, *Brewers' Guide, 1898*, 66; Williamson, *History of Western Ohio*, 613; "Trade Notes," *Beverage Journal*, January 1922, 22, https://books.google.com/books?id=guw1AQAAMAAJ.

73. "Prominent Citizen Dead," *Lima (OH) Times-Democrat*, January 24, 1902, 2.

Chapter 7

74. Author interview with Jack Waite, October 15, 2017.

75. Ohio History Central, "Greenville, Ohio," n.d., http://www.ohiohistorycentral.org/w/Greenville,_Ohio; "1794: Battle of Fallen Timbers Opens Northwest Territory to Settlement," *Native Voices*,

n.d., https://www.nlm.nih.gov/nativevoices/timeline/243.html; Jeff Puterbaugh, untitled report, Greenville, OH, unpublished, n.d., Jeff Puterbaugh's collection.

76. J. Chase Jr., *Map of Darke County, Ohio* (Philadelphia, PA: S.H. Matthews, 1857), https://lccn.loc.gov/2012592229; McIntosh, *History of Darke County*, 504; Sanborn, *Greenville, August 1887*, map 2; "The County Options Elections in Ohio," *The Western Brewer*, November 1908, 588, https://books.google.com/books?id=Hus1AQAAMAAJ&pg=PA588.

77. Andrew Olson, "The Bee Line Railroad: At the Dawn of the Midwest Railroad Era," *Indiana History Blog*, http://blog.history.in.gov/?p=1931; McIntosh, *History of Darke County*, 395–96; E. Tucker, *History of Randolph County, Indiana* (Chicago: A.L. Kingman, 1882), 437, 438, 440; C.S. Warner, L.C. Warner and C.A.O. McClellan, *Map of Randolph County, Indiana* (Waterloo City, IN: C.A.O. McClellan, 1865), https://lccn.loc.gov/2013593178.

78. Ned Bleuer and Deborah DeChurch, *Flat, but Not Dull: Understanding the Central Indiana Glacial Landscape* (Bloomington: Indiana Geological and Water Survey, Indiana University, 2017), https://igws.indiana.edu/Surficial/CentralIndiana.cfm.

79. D.J. Lake and B.N. Griffing, *Atlas of Darke County, Ohio* (Philadelphia, PA: Lake, Griffing & Stevenson, 1875), 18; "Wanted—to Sell Out," *Cincinnati Daily Star*, April 13, 1876, 1; business card, Louie's Place, Bradford, OH, Louis Willaume.

80. Erik Martin, "Lincoln Funeral Train Passage Commemorated in New Madison," *Greenville Daily Advocate*, July 4, 2017, n.p., http://www.dailyadvocate.com/news/36276/lincoln-funeral-train-passage-commemorated-in-new-madison.

81. Lake and Griffing, *Atlas of Darke County*, 63; Glenn Hindsley, *Events of Yesteryears of New Madison, Ohio* (Greenville, OH: Darke County Genealogical Society, 2001), 22; "Fatal," article from unknown newspaper, n.d., *Scrapbook of Darke Co., Ohio People*, 34.

Chapter 8

82. ONRA, "Madonna of the Trail," http://www.ohionationalroad.org/madonna_of_the_trail; William M. Rockel, *20th Century History of Springfield and Clark County, Ohio* (Chicago: Biographical Publishing Company, 1908), 158, 366, 374, 434.

83. Benjamin F. Prince, *A Standard History of Springfield and Clark County, Ohio*, vol. 1 (Chicago: American Historical Society, 1922), 54, https://books.google.com/books?id=hToVAAAAYAAJ; Beers, *History of Clark County*, 1881, 546; Howe, *Historical Collections*, 1:395, 696.

84. Charles Marvin Vorce, *Genealogical and Historical Record*, 1906, 2–3, 25, https://books.google.com/books?id=SghaAAAAMAAJ; will of Silas A. Vorce, "Ohio, Wills and Probate Records, 1786–1998," vols. 3–4, 1855–73, Ancestry.com, https://www.ancestry.com/interactive/8801/00543 0724_00148?pid=15259399; "Springfield Brewery!" *Springfield Republic*, October 7, 1861, 2; Rockel, *20ᵗʰ Century History*, 401.

85. Salem, *Beer*, 244.

86. Mira Wilkins, *The History of Foreign Investment in the United States to 1914* (Cambridge, MA: Harvard University Press, 1989), 298–99, 324–25, 331; "Springfield Breweries," *The Economist*, March 29, 1890, 403; Wahl and Henius, *Brewers' Guide*, 1898, 69.

87. "New Corporations," *National Corporation Reporter*, August 17, 1905, 1,004, https://books.google.com/books?id=U9BPAQAAIAAJ; "Brewery Items," *Ice and Refrigeration*, September 1905, 119; "Brewery Refrigeration," *Industrial Refrigeration*, October 1905, 154, https://books.google.com/books?id=1-E1AQAAMAAJ.

88. Rockel, *20ᵗʰ Century History*, 745, 198, 199; Ohio Masonic Home, "About Us," http://www.ohiomasonichome.org/about-us.

Chapter 9

89. *Primary Documents in American History*, "18ᵗʰ Amendment to the U.S. Constitution" (Washington, D.C.: Library of Congress, 2017), https://www.loc.gov/rr/program/bib/ourdocs/18thamendment.html; William Rufus Day, *U.S. Reports: Hawke v. Smith, 253 U.S. 221* (1920), Washington, D.C.: Library of Congress, n.d., https://www.loc.gov/item/usrep253221; Ballotpedia, "Ohio Prohibition on Alcohol, Amendment 2 (1918)," n.d., https://ballotpedia.org/Ohio_Prohibition_on_Alcohol,_Amendment_2_(1918).

90. Ernest H. Cherrington, *The Evolution of Prohibition in the United States of America* (Westerville, OH: American Issue Press, 1920), 17, 93–95; J. Wadsworth, ed., *The Templar's Magazine* 1 (1851), Order of the Temple of Honor, https://books.google.com/books?id=HytJAQAAMAAJ; "Jehu," *Random House Kernerman Webster's College Dictionary*, 2010, https://www.thefreedictionary.com/Jehu.

NOTES TO PAGES 149–154

91. Dio Lewis, "Introduction," in Reverend W.C. Steel, *The Woman's Temperance Movement* (New York: National Temperance Society and Publication House, 1874), 36, 325, 327, 329–30, 301–302, 305, https://books.google.com/books?id=oysAPglNoAkC; Reverend J.W. Klise, *The County of Highland* [Ohio] (Madison, WI: Northwestern Historical Association, 1902), 160, https://books.google.com/books?id=3DsVAAAAYAAJ.

92. Eliza Daniel Stewart, *Memories of the Crusade* (Chicago: H.J. Smith & Company, 1890), 78, https://books.google.com/books?id=lH1DAAAAIAAJ; Frances Elizabeth Willard and Mary Ashton Rice Livermore, *A Woman of the Century* (Buffalo, NY: Charles Wells Moulton, 1893), 687–88, https://books.google.com/books?id=zXEEAAAAYAAJ&pg=PA687.

93. Jim Sayre, "Temperance Movement Had Roots in Shelby County, Ohio," Traveling through Time, Shelby County Historical Society, http://www.shelbycountyhistory.org/schs/archives/women/cnationwomena.htm; Carry Amelia Nation, *The Use and Need of the Life of Carry A. Nation* (Topeka, KS: F.M. Steves & Sons, 1909), 61–62, 65–67, https://books.google.com/books?id=PLdIAAAAYAAJ.

94. State Historical Society of Missouri, "Carry A. Nation," Historic Missourians, n.d., https://shsmo.org/historicmissourians/name/n/nation; "Gentle Was the Sensational and Erratic Carrie Nation during Her Brief Sojourn in the Gem City," *Dayton Daily News*, September 26, 1904, 12; "Ross Impersonated Carrie Nation on Third Street and Soon Landed in a Cell in the Central Station," *Dayton Daily News*, October 24, 1904, 3.

95. Adam Schantz, "An Appeal to Reason," *Dayton Daily News*, December 23, 1907, 8–9; "Industrial Importance of the Brewer's Art" and "Prohibition Will Not Solve the Problem," *Dayton Journal*, June 21, 1908, 6, 7.

96. Albert Lieber, "Report of the Vigilance Committee," *Proceedings of the Forty-Eighth Convention* (New York: United States Brewers' Association, 1908), https://books.google.com/books?id=7hNRAQAAMAAJ; "The Ohio Dry Campaign of 1917," ehistory, https://ehistory.osu.edu/exhibitions/ohiodry/default; Harvey C. Smith, *Annual Report of the Secretary of State to the Governor and General Assembly of the State of Ohio for the Year Ending June 30, 1920*, Internet Archives, https://archive.org/details/annualreportsec26statgoog/page/n4.

97. "Turned into a Bottling Works," *Dayton Daily News*, January 3, 1906, 9; "Breweries Closed," *American Brewers' Review*, December 1908, 631, https://books.google.com/books?id=ZyIyAQAAMAAJ; W.J. Rorabaugh, *Prohibition: A Concise History* (New York: Oxford University Press, 2018), 53.

98. "Brewing Plants Will Suspend Work Saturday," *Dayton Daily News*, August 16, 1918, 10; "Breweries, Built at Original Cost of $425,000 Sold," *Dayton Daily News*, September 23, 1919, 13; "Cleveland Firm Acquires Local Brewery Plant," *Dayton Journal*, November 5, 1919, n.p.; advertisement, "The Following Materials Are for Sale," *Dayton Daily News*, November 13, 1919, 13; "Undermine Huge Stack for Fall," *Dayton Daily News*, November 10, 1920, 13; legal notice, "Master Commissioner's Sale of Real Estate in Dayton, Ohio," *Dayton Daily News*, October 10, 1921, 20.
99. "Prohibition Put Home City Brewing on Hold," *Springfield News-Sun*, March 17, 2007, A4; "Old Brewery Building on W. Main Being Wrecked," *Springfield News-Sun*, July 14, 1974, 9.
100. "Brewery Plans to Make Soft Drinks," *Dayton Daily News*, May 24, 1919, 14.

Chapter 10

101. Author interview with Kevin Loftis, October 27, 2017; Kirsten Dangaran et al., *Economic Impact of Ohio's Craft Beer Industry, 2015* (Columbus: Ohio State University Fisher College of Business, December 2016), 4, https://www.ohiocraftbeer.org/wp-content/uploads/2016/01/EconomicImpactFinalreportwithAppendix2.pdf.
102. Ohio Craft Brewers Association, "Ohio Craft Beer Facts," https://www.ohiocraftbeer.org/about-ocba.
103. "A Taste for Success: Taprooms Have Been a Real Boon for Area Craft Brewers," *Toledo Blade*, June 8, 2014, https://www.toledoblade.com/Culture/2014/06/08/A-taste-for-success-Taprooms-have-been-a-real-boon-for-area-craft-brewers; Kevin J. Gray, "Will Dayton Finally See Locally Produced Beer Again?" *Dayton City Paper*, August 2, 2011, http://www.daytoncitypaper.com/will-dayton-finally-see-locally-produced-beer-again.
104. Author interview with Nate Cornett and Lisa Wolters, October 27, 2017.
105. Mark Fisher, "Brewing Up Anticipation Around the Dayton Region," *Dayton Daily News*, January 19, 2018, Go-8; Mark Fisher, "Will the Local Brewpub Bubble Burst?" *Dayton Daily News*, December 29, 2013, Business-1.
106. News release, "The Wandering Griffin Collaborates to Produce Limited Edition Beer," Beavercreek Chamber of Commerce, July 18, 2017, https://

www.beavercreekchamber.org/news/details/the-wandering-griffin-collaborates-to-produce-limited-edition-beer; Cecilia Fox and Belinda M. Paschal, "What's Brewing Around the Valley," *Piqua Daily Call*, October 14, 2018, https://www.dailycall.com/news/47526/whats-brewing-around-the-valley; author interview with Steve Barnhart, September 1, 2017.

107. Author interview with Brad Bergefurd, October 27, 2017; author interview with Jamie Arthur, July 29, 2017.

108. "Five Questions with Glenn Perrine," *Akron Beacon Journal*, June 17, 2016, https://www.ohio.com/akron/pages/five-questions-with-glenn-perrine.

ABOUT THE AUTHOR

Timothy R. Gaffney is a writer and author who was born in Dayton in 1951 and has lived in the Miami Valley most of his life. After earning a bachelor's degree from The Ohio State University in Columbus in 1974, he worked for the *Piqua Daily Call*, the *Kettering-Oakwood Times* and the *Dayton Daily News*. He is the author of sixteen books. He is director of communications for the National Aviation Heritage Area and a volunteer trustee for the United States Air and Trade Show Inc., producer of the Dayton Air Show. His interests include flying, photography, bicycling and hiking. He dabbled in homebrewing until he got tired of washing bottles. He lives in Miamisburg, Ohio, with his wife, Jean. They have four grown children, two grandchildren and two dogs.